REVEL

A Liturgical Prophecy

Revelation

A LITURGICAL PROPHECY

Patrick Henry Reardon

ST VLADIMIR'S SEMINARY PRESS
YONKERS, NEW YORK
2018

Library of Congress Cataloging-in-Publication Data

Names: Reardon, Patrick Henry, 1938- author.
Title: Revelation : a liturgical prophecy / by Patrick Henry Reardon.
Description: Yonkers, NY : St. Vladimirs Seminary Press, 2018.
Identifiers: LCCN 2018030024 (print) | LCCN 2018031341 (ebook) | ISBN
    9780881416381 | ISBN 9780881416374 (alk. paper)
Subjects: LCSH: Bible. Revelation—Commentaries.
Classification: LCC BS2825.53 (ebook) | LCC BS2825.53 .R425 2018 (print) | DDC
    228/.07—dc23
LC record available at https://lccn.loc.gov/2018030024

Translations of Scripture and of all ancient or modern texts are by
the author. References to the Psalms are given first according to
the Hebrew numbering, and then in parentheses according to the
Septuagint enumeration.

COPYRIGHT © 2018 BY
ST VLADIMIR'S SEMINARY PRESS
575 Scarsdale Road, Yonkers, NY 10707
1-800-204-2665
www.svspress.com

ISBN 978-0-88141-637-4 (print)
ISBN 978-0-88141-638-1 (electronic)

Table of Contents

INTRODUCTION

This most difficult and mysterious book—"*le livre le plus difficile de tout le Nouveau Testament*," wrote André Feuillet—was written most likely near the end of the first century and in the context of the persecution of the Christian Church by the Emperor Domitian (reigned AD 81–96). The work is especially concerned with the events of the Last Times and is the largest work of prophecy to come to us from early Christianity. It is dominated by the vision of the risen Christ living and walking among the churches as they do battle with Satan in this world. After epistles to seven local churches in Asia Minor, it records a series of visions and angelic messages crafted in very elaborate and often difficult symbolism.

This is no book for biblical beginners, and one suspects it is a work more often misinterpreted than correctly understood. Unless a person is extraordinarily familiar with all the rest of Holy Scripture, understanding very much of the Book of Revelation will be an extremely arduous task. I dare to hope—barely—that the present commentary may prove helpful.

Since the book's arcane symbolism is so rich and subtle, Christian humility will especially prompt the devout reader to be more than usually careful and tentative in his study of it, bearing in mind that the book's purpose is not to satisfy our curiosity about the final times (inasmuch as not even the angels in heaven—and therefore certainly no one on earth—truly know the day and hour, as our Lord insisted in the Gospels) but to summon our ongoing repentance.

Addressed to seven specific churches of Asia, Revelation also resembles the Epistle to the Hebrews, which is really a sermon composed for public reading. Like Hebrews, too, Revelation has much to say about the heavenly sanctuary. Still, the many differences between these two works are manifest. In short, the Book of Revelation is unique, in the sense that no other book of Holy Scripture is entirely like it.

This does not mean, however, that biblical literature provides no analogues to the Book of Revelation. Indeed, its close analysis leads the present interpreter to approach this as a work of "liturgical prophecy," a prophetic word to be delivered in the context of the Church's sacramental and liturgical worship.

This description of the book, accordingly, has two parts, corresponding to the noun "prophecy" and the adjective "liturgical." We will take these in turn.

[1]Unlike the rest of the New Testament, the Book of Revelation is not read liturgically in the Orthodox Church: it is never appointed as the reading preceding the gospel in the Divine Liturgy (as the Book of Acts and all the Pauline and General Epistles are throughout the course of the annual lectionary), nor is it ever read after the prokeimenon in Great Vespers (as the General Epistles are read for the feasts of certain apostles, though this is otherwise a place for readings from the Old Testament). While it is true that the Typikon calls for the entire New Testament (apart from the Gospels and *including* Revelation) to be read over the course of the year after the artoklasia at the vigil, this practice has fallen out of use everywhere.

The status of the Book of Revelation was unresolved for many centuries, but by the eighth century it was accepted universally in the Church. It had always found supporters in the previous centuries: St Ireneaeus—who knew St Polycarp (d. AD 156), who in turn knew the author of Revelation—accepted the work as canonical; the Muratorian Fragment (*c.* 170) includes it in its canon; St Athanasius (*c.* 298–373) includes it in his list of biblical books in *Epistle 39*; St Andrew of Caesarea (563–637) both accepted Revelation and wrote an influential commentary on it; and St John of Damascus (*c.* 675–749) accepts its canonical status in *An Exact Exposition of the Orthodox Faith* 4.7.—*Ed.*

Prophecy

Let us begin with the noun "prophecy." To the average reader of Revelation, it will be obvious that Revelation is a prophetic book. After all, it explicitly calls itself this. "Blessed is he who reads and those who hear the words of this *prophecy*," the author says, near the book's very beginning (1.3). Again, four times in the final chapter the book uses the word "prophecy" to describe itself: "Blessed is he who keeps the words of the *prophecy* of this book" (22.7); "Do not seal the words of the *prophecy* of this book, for the time is at hand" (22.10); "For I testify to everyone who hears the words of the *prophecy* of this book. If anyone adds to these things, God will add to him the plagues that are written in this book; and if anyone takes away the words of the book of this *prophecy*, God will take away his part in the Book of Life" (22.18–19). In addition, references to the prophets are found seven times throughout the book (10.7; 11.8; 16.6; 18.20, 24; 22.6, 9).

Why, then, am I making such a point of insisting that the Book of Revelation should be treated as prophetic? What prompts me to urge the obvious?

I do so in order to establish the principles and procedures by which we interpret the work. If the Book of Revelation is truly a prophetic work, then we should go about understanding it in very much the way we go about understanding the other biblical prophets, such as Isaiah, Jeremiah, or Amos. That is to say, we begin by placing the Book of Revelation, as far as possible, in its own historical context, in order to ascertain how the book was understood by its first readers. This is how we commence our interpretation of all the Bible's prophetic books.

Let us take, for example, the Book of Amos. I select Amos deliberately, because he was the first of the Bible's literary prophets, just as St John the Seer was the last. When we say that Amos was the Bible's original "literary prophet" we mean that he was the first biblical prophet whose extended oracles were consigned to writing in a single book. This is what distinguishes him from earlier prophets like Nathan and Elijah. In this respect Amos serves as a point of transition in the history of the sacred canon.

Writing down and preserving of prophetic utterances was arguably the most distinctive contribution of eighth century Israel. The very act of transcribing God's oracles manifested a different perspective, a new awareness that the prophetic message possessed a permanent relevance beyond the circumstances of its original time and place. The prophecies of Nathan in the tenth century and of Elijah in the ninth were spoken into the air, and they disappeared like any other spoken word. The narratives of the Books of Samuel and Kings preserve but the scraps of what the prophets said.

Someone in the eighth century, however, perhaps Amos himself, believed that his prophetic message had a timeless significance. In the course of criticizing the economic, political, social, and religious situation of his age, Amos was perceived to be making important comments applicable to all other ages to come. There arose the conviction that his words were worth recording for future generations. The origin of the Book of Amos lay in that conviction. Amos marked the transition from prophecy to prophetic literature.

At the same time, it is important to observe that the Book of Amos does not begin on this note of its timelessness. The future validity of the words of Amos was not based on some abstract integrity perceived to be characteristic of his thought. His words were not preserved because his contemporaries perceived a high and compelling philosophical coherence in his message. His message was profoundly validated to his contemporaries, rather, by the plain fact that what he predicted came to pass, thus proving that he was right. In denouncing the sins of Israel during the reign of Jeroboam II, Amos had foretold the impending downfall of Samaria. And this downfall, which took place in 722, demonstrated that the words of Amos were worth taking seriously. He had not only prophesied that event; he had also analyzed the social and religious causes that brought it about.

In other words, when history demonstrated that Amos was accurate in his assessment of the outcome, his contemporaries understood him to be accurate in his assessment of the cause. When his historical foresight was shown to be correct, then one had to conclude that his historical insight was correct. His foresight validated his insight.

The Book of Amos commences, therefore, with an explicit reference to his timeframe. Those ancient editors who placed the Book of Amos in the Bible were very careful to tell us that he prophesied "in the days of Uzziah king of Judah, and in the days of Jeroboam the son of Joash king of Israel." This priceless historical information about Amos stands at the beginning of the text in order to send us to the Books of Kings, so that we will understand the context in which the prophet spoke to his contemporaries in the eighth century before Christ. Amos' words of prophecy, that is to say, are not timeless except by being timely. Those words are valid for all of history precisely because their interpretive connection with an individual part of history.

Thus, the Bible prohibits us from reading Amos as a work of theoretical abstraction. His own book obliges us to read him first in the context of his own place and time. Before asking what Amos' words mean to us, the Bible compels us first to ask what those words meant to his contemporaries. We must go back to the eighth century before Christ and examine the social, political, economic, and religious context that Amos was prophetically addressing. This is why the opening of the Book of Amos implicitly sends us to the Books of Kings.

Salvation and History

Moreover, the very structure of the Sacred Canon is instructive on this point. We are touching here on the reason why some of the Bible's historical books were canonically placed at the beginning of the prophetic writings. The books of Joshua, Judges, Samuel, and Kings form that part of the Hebrew Bible known as the "former prophets." This designation indicates that these historical books are read first, because they provide the necessary context for reading the next section of the canon, namely, the "latter prophets." The "latter prophets" include, of course, Isaiah, Jeremiah, Ezekiel, and the twelve "minor prophets." Thus, what we think of as the Bible's prophetic books are rendered inseparable from the context of its historical books. The biblical prophets are not allowed to become mere philosophers.

In this respect, it is worth calling attention to the parallel case with the Torah, the *Chumash*, the "Five Fifths of the Law." The literary structure of the Pentateuch places the giving of God's Law within an elaborate and detailed historical context. What God said to Israel through Moses on Mount Sinai is inseparable from the historical circumstances in which he said it. The stories in Genesis, Exodus, and Numbers provide the particulars of that context. Thus, Torah is never reduced to a universal theory. That is to say, it is pertinent to all of history precisely because it first touches a particular part of history. The text is ever contextualized by time and place.

In varying degrees this same principle is characteristic of all the biblical prophets. Most of the prophetic books of Holy Scripture tell us when the prophet spoke. Thus, we learn that Isaiah was called "in the year that King Uzziah died" (742 BC) and that his long ministry lasted through "the days of Uzziah, Jotham, Ahaz, and Hezechiah, kings of Judah." Similarly, at the beginning of the Book of Jeremiah, we are informed that he prophesied "in the days of Josiah the son of Amon, king of Judah, in the thirteenth year of his reign" (Jer 1.2). Ezekiel, likewise, tells us that he received his inaugural vision "in the fifth year of King Jehoiachin's captivity" (Ez 1.2). Haggai begins his message "in the second year of King Darius, in the sixth month, on the first day of the month" (Hag 1.1). Two months later, Zechariah commences his prophecy "in the eighth month of the second year of King Darius" (Zech 1.1). Over and over again, the Bible's prophetic books, whether explicitly or by implication, set the oracles of God into specified historical contexts, contexts that indicate how we are to interpret and understand them. To repeat, biblical prophecy is not universal except by being particular; it does not become timeless except by being timely.

Now this feature is true of prophecy because it is true of salvation. Jesus is the Savior of the whole world, because he "suffered under Pontius Pilate." The most significant, and the only salvific, event in all of human history is linked to a particular moment in history, explicitly documented.

The gospel itself is timeless only by being timely. Christian salvation does not consist in finding a universal religious truth outside of time, but in discovering the particular place where eternity enters time. Namely, when the Word became flesh and dwelt among us. The beginning of the gospel takes place, St Luke tells us:

> in the fifteenth year of the reign of Tiberius Caesar, Pontius Pilate being governor of Judea, Herod being tetrarch of Galilee, his brother Philip being tetrarch of Iturea and the region of Trachonitis, and Lysanias tetrarch of Abilene, during the high priesthood of Annas and Caiaphas. (Luke 3.1–2)

Immediacy

With respect to the Bible's prophetic books, from the beginning this truth has served as a hermeneutic principle for their correct interpretation. It is a sound principle, I submit, indicated by the Bible itself. This is why I have begun by insisting that the Book of Revelation is a prophetic book, and it should be treated the same way we treat the other prophetic books.

In order to understand the Apocalypse correctly, it is imperative to inquire how it was understood by those who first read it and heard it read. If our own understanding is to be valid, it must be related to that original understanding of the first Christian readers. After all, this is the same rule that we employ for the other books in the New Testament. We would not think of interpreting the epistles to the Galatians and the Corinthians without regard to the immediate context of those two churches. To attempt such a thing would be to do violence to the epistles themselves. The same is true of the Book of Revelation.

Let me suggest that this approach to the Book of Revelation enjoys the advantage of avoiding a lot of exegetical nonsense. After all, the early Christians at Thyatira and Philadelphia would never have preserved a work that they did not understand. It is not as though those ancient Christians, on reading the Book of Revelation for the first time, sat around, scratching their heads in vain, completely stymied by what it meant.

We should not think of the believers at Sardis and Pergamum as saying among themselves. "Well, we can't make heads or tails of any of this. I mean, who knows how to figure out this 666 business or explain the thousand year reign of the saints? Good grief, the last thing we needed was a complex riddle that has nothing to do with our own lives. Why has our beloved John suddenly taken to speaking in riddles? We haven't the foggiest idea what all this stuff means. But just to be safe, let's make lots of copies of this book and send it out to the other churches. Maybe somebody out there will have clue. Who knows? There may be someone able to figure out this puzzle over the next two thousand years. Perhaps in the twentieth century or so, when world history really does go to seed, some truly wise person will sit down and write a commentary to explain it all. Heaven knows *we* have no idea what it means."

This is absurd, of course. By and large, that is to say, we must presume that the faithful at Ephesus, Smyrna, and Laodicea had some idea what John was talking about when he described his various visions. If we want to understand what the Book of Revelation means, therefore, it is imperative that we begin by investigating what its first readers *thought* it meant. The book's first readers must be our guides to an understanding of it. This is the same hermeneutic approach we take to the other prophetic books of the Bible.

Indeed, this note of immediacy is sounded several times in the course of the Apocalypse itself. It speaks of "things which must *shortly* take place" (ἃ δεῖ γενέσθαι ἐν τάχει—1.1). John's readers certainly did not think that the events predicted in this book would come to pass centuries in the distant future. They pertained, rather, to the "here and now" of their own time. That same expression— "things which must *shortly* take place" (ἃ δεῖ γενέσθαι ἐν τάχει)—is found again near the end of the book (22.6). In John's visions, the perceived time is not far off. On the contrary, he tells us, "the time is near" (ὁ γὰρ καιρὸς ἐγγύς—1.3). This same theme comes again at the end of the book: "the time is near" (ὁ καιρὸς γὰρ ἐγγύς ἐστιν—22.10).

Warning and Repentance

In fact, the immediate context of the Book of Revelation is not terribly hard to detect. The seven letters to the seven churches of Asia, in Chapters 2 and 3, show that the book is essentially a prophetic call to repentance in the face of an impending and expected persecution of Christians by elements of the Roman state. The ensuing chapters describe this coming persecution in a series of scenes arranged according to the number seven: seven seals, seven trumpets, seven bowls of plagues. Each scene of each section in this series appears to describe exactly what is described in the corresponding scene in the other sections. All of these scenes represent a summons to repentance. Thus, the Book of Revelation is a long prophecy in the sense of a repeated warning.

The first Christian readers of this book were expected to know exactly what it meant and exactly what they were expected to do about it. That is to say, the Book of Revelation is not a treasury of information about things to come in the distant future. It was a very practical book, calling for a very practical response.

As a prophetic warning, the Book of Revelation may be compared to other parts of the New Testament. For example, there is Acts 11.27–30, where the prophet Agabus "stood up and showed by the Spirit that there was going to be a great famine throughout all the world, which happened in the days of Claudius Caesar." This was not a prediction of some distant catastrophe; it was, rather, a proximate matter that the Christians at Antioch could actually do something about.

The earliest Christians seemed to have relied a great deal on such prophecies, which served as admonitions about impending events that affected the Church in some way. Thus, that same Agabus later appears in Acts 21.10–11, to warn the apostle Paul of his imminent arrest by the Jews and his handing over to the Gentiles. We know the names of other individual prophets, such as Judas and Silas of Jerusalem (Acts 15.31). There are further references to anonymous prophets elsewhere in the New Testament (Eph 2.20; 4.11).

A very striking instance of such a prophetic warning was left us by Eusebius of Caesarea. He tells us that, at the time of Vespasian's conquest of the Holy Land, "the people of the church in Jerusalem were commanded by an oracle (κατά τινα χρησμὸν), given by revelation (δὶ ἀποκαλύψεως) to certain approved men there before the war, to leave the city and to abide in a certain town of Perea called Pella."[2] Because of this prophetic warning that they received, few or no Christians perished during the two years' siege and the downfall of Jerusalem to Titus in the year 70.

In the case of the Book of Revelation, John's apocalyptic admonition is not a call to flee, but a summons to repent. This theme appears repeatedly in the letters to the seven churches. "*Repent* and do the former works, or else I will come to you quickly, and remove your lamp stand from its place, unless you repent" (2.5); "*Repent*, or else I will come to you quickly and fight against them with the sword of my mouth" (2.16); "And I gave her time to *repent* of her fornication, and she did not *repent*. Indeed, I will cast her into a sickbed, and those who commit adultery with her into great tribulation, unless they *repent* of their deeds" (2.21–22); "Remember, therefore, how you have received and heard; hold fast and *repent*" (3.3); "As many as I love, I chasten. Therefore, be zealous and *repent*" (3.19). Six of the seven Asian churches are commanded to repent. The exception is the faithful church at Philadelphia, which is simply told, "Behold, I am coming quickly! Hold fast to what you have, that no one may take your crown" (3.11).

The traditional view is that the coming crisis envisaged in the Book of Revelation was the expected persecution of Christians toward the end of the reign of Emperor Domitian (81–96). Our

[2]Eusebius, *Ecclesiastical History* 3.5.3.

earliest witness for this view, in fact, was a churchman intimately familiar with the Asian churches, Irenaeus of Lyons, an immediate associate of Polycarp, the bishop of Smyrna.[3]

Later exegetes have challenged this tradition by suggesting that the impending crisis reflected in this book was, at least partly, the persecution of Nero in the mid-60s. As far as we know from primary sources, however, Nero's persecution affected only the Christians at Rome, not in the rest of the empire. Although some of the imagery in the Book of Revelation does seem to reflect themes associated with Nero, it is my own view that the traditional opinion is the correct one.

In a deeper sense, nonetheless, the specific settling of this historical question is not ultimately decisive. The book itself testifies sufficiently to its purpose, which was to prepare several of the ancient Christian churches, those in Asia Minor, for an impending persecution from the official Roman authorities. What these churches needed chiefly to do was to repent.

As a work of biblical prophecy, therefore, the Apocalypse is an exhortation to repentance. It is not a handbook of eschatological curiosity. It does not convey new information, as it were, about the events leading up to the end time. It is not a work of cryptography, a kind of eschatological Rohrschach test. It is a waste of time, and therefore a failure in stewardship, to treat the Book of Revelation as a symbolic, coded narrative about human history during the final ages of the world. The Book of Revelation provides not the slightest new information about specific political or cosmic events taking place in any century except the first century, the life-time of its first readers.

Indeed, to treat the Apocalypse as providing esoteric information about the final times of history is to violate another biblical mandate directed against such speculation. In one of his last words immediately prior to his ascension into heaven, Jesus admonished us, "It is not for you to know the times and seasons which the Father has put in his own authority" (Acts 1.7). "Of that day and hour," he

---

[3]Irenaeus of Lyons, *Against the Heresies* 5.30.3.

reminded us, "no one knows, not even the angels of heaven, but my Father only" (Mt 24.36). "Watch, therefore, for you know neither the day nor the hour in which the Son of Man is coming" (Mt 25.13).

This exhortatory theme was taken up by the Apostle Paul in his very first epistle. "But concerning times and seasons, brethren, you have no need that I should write to you. For you yourselves know perfectly that the day of the Lord so comes as a thief in the night" (1 Thess 5.1). We should presume, therefore, that the Book of Revelation did not become a part of Holy Scripture for the purpose of inciting a curiosity that Holy Scripture everywhere else tells us not to indulge.

Liturgical Setting

I began by describing the Book of Revelation as a work of liturgical prophecy. We must now turn to a consideration of that adjective, "liturgical."

The book's liturgical setting is indicated in its very first chapter. "I was in the Spirit *on the Lord's Day*" (ἐν τῇ κυριακῇ ἡμέρᾳ—1.10). The seer is in prayer. And because he is in prayer, he is facing East. Just to the East of where he stands in prayer lies the western shore of Asia, where John in mystic vision beholds the ring of the seven churches. They are lamp stands, forming a sort of Menorah. "I saw seven golden lamp stands," he wrote, and he is told, "the seven golden lamp stands which you saw are the seven churches" (1.12, 20).

And just what are these seven churches doing "on the Lord's Day"? We know from 1 Corinthians 16.2 that the Christians gathered on the first day of the week, or, more literally, "*day one* of the week" (κατὰ μίαν σαββάτου). This is the identical expression used in Genesis (1.5) to describe "day one" of Creation, יוֹם אֶחָד:, or ἡμέρα μία. This striking expression is also used to refer to the day of the Lord's Resurrection. The women came to the tomb, say Mark and Luke, τῇ μιᾷ τῶν σαββάτων, literally "*day one* of the week" (Mk 16.1; Lk 24.1).

So, once again, what are these seven churches doing on the day commemorating both creation and the resurrection? As described in the Acts of the Apostles (20.7–11) and Pliny's famous letter to Trajan, [4] they spent the whole night in prayer, and now they are gathered in the Eucharistic worship, known as the Breaking of the Bread. Thus, we read in the *Didache* (14.1), "Gathering on the Lord's Day (κατὰ κυριακὴν δὲ Κυρίου), break the Bread and give thanks (κλάσατε ἄρτον καὶ εὐχαριστήσατε)."

[4] Pliny, *Letters* 10.96.

23

The Book of Revelation is our first witness to the expression "the Lord's day," which became a technical term that referred to the day after the Sabbath. It was that first day of the week, on which God made both Lord and Christ that Jesus who was crucified (Acts 2.36). The "Lord's day" very early replaced the Jewish Sabbath as the chief day of the week, therefore, when the Church gathered to celebrate the resurrection of the Lord.

Thus, not much beyond a decade after the Book of Revelation, Ignatius of Antioch wrote that "those who had walked in the ancient practices attained to newness of hope, no longer observing Sabbaths (μηκέτι σαββατίζοντες), but living according to the Lord's Day (κατὰ κυριακὴν ζῶντες), on which our life also rose with him and through his death."[5]

Again, we have the testimony of Dionysius of Corinth only a few decades later. "Today we observe the holy Day of the Lord (κυριακὴν ἁγίαν ἡμέραν διηγάγομεν)."[6] Among the Asian Fathers themselves, we know that Melito, the bishop of Sardis in the mid-second century wrote a treatise entitled Περὶ κυριακῆς, "On the Lord's Day."[7]

This expression, "the Lord's Day," however, was of significance only to those inside the Church. When Christians addressed those outside the Church, they spoke of this day by its pagan reference, "the day of the sun," or Sunday. Thus, Justin Martyr, giving Antoninus Pius his famous description of the eucharistic worship of the Christian Church, said that it took place "on the day called the day of the sun" (τῇ τοῦ ἡλίου λεγομένῃ ἡμέρᾳ).[8]

It is most significant that John's mystic visions are expressly tied to that specific day on which Christians celebrated those sacred mysteries in which earth and heaven are joined. This is the day on which Christians gather at the throne of God. This is the day on which they draw nigh

[5]Ignatius of Antioch, *Magnesians* 9.1.
[6]Eusebius, *Ecclesiastical History* 4.23.11.
[7]*Ibid* 4.26.2.
[8]Justin Martyr, *First Apology* 67.

> to Mount Zion and to the city of the living God, the heavenly
> Jerusalem, to an innumerable company of angels, to the gen-
> eral assembly and church of the firstborn who are registered in
> heaven, to God the judge of all, to the spirits of just men made
> perfect, to Jesus the mediator of the new covenant, and to the
> blood of sprinkling that speaks better things than that of Abel.
> (Hebrews 12.22–24)

The Book of Revelation describes every one of these components
listed in the Epistle to the Hebrews: the innumerable company of
angels, the sacrificial blood of the mediating Christ, the spirits of
the just men made perfect, the general assembly and church of the
firstborn, and Mount Zion, the new city, the heavenly Jerusalem. The
visions of the Book of Revelation take us into that tabernacle not
made with hands, complete with the golden censer and the ark of
the covenant overlaid on all sides with gold, wherein was the golden
pot that had manna (Heb 9.4; Rev 2.17; 8.3; 11.19).

John portrays for us the heavenly throne of God. This very
image, God's throne, appears forty-six times in Revelation (the next
closest count in the New Testament being Matthew, where the divine
throne is found only five times).

And what happens at the throne of God? Incessant worship. John
beholds the adoration of the four living creatures, the innumerable
company of angels, the four-and-twenty elders, and all the saints,
whose number "was ten thousand times ten thousand, and thousands of thousands" (5.11). This worship in heaven, however, also
incorporates the worship of the Church on earth. We are told that
the four-and-twenty elders have "golden bowls full of incense, which
are the prayers of the saints" (5.8).

Now it is remarkable that the prayers of the saints on earth are
being offered before the throne by the saints in heaven. These four-
and-twenty elders surely correspond to the twenty-four courses of
priests in the temple, as described in I Chronicles. That is to say, these
heavenly elders are priestly figures, who are charged with offering

to God the prayers of the saints on earth. This is a striking image of the union of the Church praying on earth with the Church praying in heaven.

But this worship of the saints on earth is also assumed into the ministry of the angels. Thus, we read that "another angel, having a golden censer, came and stood at the altar. He was given much incense, that he should offer it with the prayers of all the saints upon the golden altar which was before the throne. And the smoke of the incense, with the prayers of the saints, ascended before God from the angel's hand" (8.3–4).

And when this incense is poured out on the altar, all manner of things begin to happen on earth in response to the prayers of the saints. John hears the sounding of the seven trumpets, those liturgical trumpets that in older days brought low the walls of Jericho (Josh 8.7–21; 11.15). Although the Christians are about to be persecuted by the Roman authorities, God's throne is still sovereign over all of history, and Christians still have access to that sovereign throne.

Liturgical Proclamation

As John gazes eastward, facing the rising sun, he sees One "like the Son of Man," adorned in those vestments prescribed for Aaron and his sons, "clothed in a garment down to the feet and girded about the chest with a golden band" (1.13; cf. Ex 28.4; 39.29). The sacrificed and risen Christ stands in the very midst of the lamp stands. "I am he who lives, and was dead, and behold I am alive forever more" (1.18). John is about to witness the inner secrets of what is taking place on that Sunday morning among those seven churches gathered in worship.

Moreover, John is told to inscribe what he sees, in order that what he writes may be read to those churches. "Write the things that you have seen, and the things which are, and the things which will take place after this" (1.19). When John writes, he is not thinking of a distant audience many centuries later. He is told, rather, "What you see, write in a book and send it to the seven churches that are in Asia" (1.11). When the book reaches these churches, it will be read aloud in their assemblies. "Blessed is he who reads and those who hear the words of this prophecy" (1.3). The word to "read" here is ἀναγινώσκων, which more properly means to read out loud, to proclaim. It is the verb that Luke employs to describe Jesus reading the Scriptures in the synagogue at Nazareth (Lk 4.16). It is the same word used by the Apostle Paul, when he speaks of "Moses, read every Sabbath" (Acts 15.11). Or again, still referring to the services at the synagogue, he uses the expression, "whenever Moses is read" (ἡνίκα ἂν ἀναγινώσκηται Μωυσῆς—2 Cor 3.15). The context of this expression, in other words, is the assembly of worship.

Indeed, this is the same verb that Paul employs with reference to the reading of his own epistles (cf. 2 Cor 1.13; 3.2; Eph 3.4). This is true of his very first letter, which he closes by saying, "I charge you by the Lord that this epistle be read (ἀναγνωσθῆναι) to all the holy brethren" (1 Thess 5.27). When the congregations received these epistles, they read them during the time of worship, along with the readings from the Law and the Prophets. It was an apostolic practice that the Christian churches have continued ever since. Copies of the epistles were made precisely so that this could be done. Thus, Paul wrote to the Colossians, "when this epistle is read (ἀναγνωσθῇ) among you, see that it is read (ἀναγνωσθῇ) also in the church of the Laodiceans, and that you likewise read (ἀναγνῶτε) the epistle from Laodicea" (Col 4.16).

As far as we can tell, almost the entire corpus of the New Testament began as exercises in public reading in church. Not more than sixty years after John wrote the Revelation, Justin Martyr described the normal Christian worship on Sunday. This worship began, he wrote, with a reading from "the memoirs of the apostles or the writings of the prophets."[9] He had earlier spoken of the apostles and "the memoirs composed by them, which are called Gospels."[10] Thus, we are certain that the Gospels, the Epistles, and the Book of Revelation were all read in the Church's gatherings of worship from the earliest times, along with the readings of the Law and the Prophets.

Indeed, it is no secret to any of us that the proclamatory reading of God's Word is an essential part of Christian worship. Even in heaven, it would seem, the Book is an integral component of the worship. "And I saw in the right hand of him who sat upon the throne, a scroll (βιβλίον) written inside and on the back, sealed with seven seals" (Rev 5.1). This scroll can only be opened by the Lion of Judah, the Lamb who stands "in the midst of the throne and of the four living creatures, and in the midst of the elders" (5.6). It can be opened by him because it has been fulfilled in him. "You are worthy to take the scroll and to open its seals; for you were slain and have redeemed us to God by your blood" (5.9).

[9]Justin Martyr, *First Apology* 67.
[10]Ibid, 65.

This scene in Revelation stands parallel to two scenes in the Gospel of Luke, one at the beginning of Jesus' public ministry and the other at the end of it. In the first, Luke portrays Jesus reading the Scriptures in the synagogue at Nazareth. "He was handed the book of the prophet Isaiah" (Lk 4.17). He concluded that reading by announcing, "Today this scripture is fulfilled in your hearing" (4.21). In the second place, Luke returns to this theme in the story of the two disciples who met the risen Jesus on the way to Emmaus. Luke tells us that, "beginning at Moses and all the prophets, he expounded (διερμήνευσεν) to them in all the Scriptures the things concerning himself" (Lk 24.27).

This biblical exegesis by the slain and risen Jesus is called an "opening" of the Scriptures. The two disciples afterwards reflect, "Did not our heart burn within us while he talked with us on the road, and while he *opened* the Scriptures to us?" (24.32) In Luke's very next scene, when Jesus meets with the other disciples, he tells us that Jesus "*opened* their understanding that they might comprehend the Scriptures" (24.45).

In the Book of Revelation, the Lamb alone may open the scroll. This scroll seems to be more than one thing. It is, first of all, the Scriptures themselves, considered as prophecy, fulfilled and therefore opened by Christ. It is also the symbol of God's own secret counsel, revealed by the action of the redeeming Christ in the world.

We note that the scroll comes from the hand of God, that right hand at which Christ sits in glory, but God does not open it. A human being must come forward and open the seals of God's own mind. This human being is the sacrificial Lamb, standing "as though slaughtered" (ὡς ἐσφαγμένον). He bears in his flesh the marks of having died, but behold he lives. His having died and risen are qualities that abide in his person as permanent characteristics of his existence and his relationship to the world. "I am he who lives, and was dead, and behold, I am alive forevermore" (1.18).

History and Worship

What, then, is John describing in all these visions? He is describing, in highly poetic form, what takes place when Christians gather for worship. They do not escape from the painful history of the world. On the contrary, they go to the very source of that history, the eternal throne of God. Surrounded by the seeming chaos of the world and the events of men, threatened by social and political forces dominated by the direction of hell, Christians are strengthened by John's vision of their worship being assumed into the very worship that takes place before God's throne.

John's many images of cosmic destruction do not eclipse nor detract from his greater attention to the source of all order, which is the sovereign throne of God. Around this throne constant worship that takes place in heaven. In the blood of Jesus, Christians take part in the worship of the heavenly sanctuary, the image that dominates both the Book of Revelation and the Epistle to the Hebrews, the two New Testament books best described as exhortations to repentance directed to Christians. It is of this divine throne, which appears forty-six times in the Apocalypse, that the Epistle to the Hebrews says, "Let us therefore come boldly to the *throne* of grace, that we may obtain mercy and grace to help in time of need" (4.16). John's visions bring the Asian believers to that single and lasting reality that remains when all else has disappeared. "And I saw a great white throne and him who sat on it, from whose face the earth and the heaven fled away. And there was found no place for them" (Rev 20.11).

And what gives Christians access to this divine throne? The sacrificial blood of Christ. This motif is sounded in both Hebrews and Revelation. In the former we are told "how much more shall the *blood* of Christ, who through the eternal Spirit offered himself

31

without spot to God, cleanse your conscience from dead works to serve the true and living God" (Heb 9.14). We come to the heavenly sanctuary, of which the Epistle to the Hebrews says:

> But Christ came as the High Priest of the good things to come, with the greater and more perfect tabernacle not made with hands, that is, not of this creation, not with the blood of goats and calves, but with his own *blood*, having obtained eternal redemption. (Hebrews 9.11–12)

This is the Jesus of whom the author of Hebrews writes. "Jesus also, that he might sanctify the people with his own *blood*, suffered outside the gate" (Heb 13.12). "Therefore, brethren," the author goes on:

> having boldness to enter the Holiest by the *blood* of Jesus, by a new and living way which he consecrated for us, through the veil, that is his flesh, and having a High Priest over the house of God, let us draw near with a true heart, in full assurance of faith, having our hearts sprinkled from an evil conscience and our bodies washed with pure water. Let us hold fast the confession of our hope without wavering, for he who promised is faithful. And let us consider one another in order to stir up love and good works, not forsaking the *assembling of ourselves together*, as is the manner of some, but exhorting one another, and so much the more as you see the Day approaching (ἐγγίζουσαν τὴν ἡμέραν). (Hebrews 10.19–25)

And in order to come "to Mount Zion and to the city of the living God, the heavenly Jerusalem, to an innumerable company of angels, to the general assembly and church of the firstborn who are registered in heaven, to God the judge of all, and to the spirits of just men made perfect" (Heb 12.22–23), we must come "to Jesus the Mediator of the new covenant, and to the *blood* of sprinkling that speaks better things than that of Abel" (12.24). The God we come to in our worship is described as "the God of peace, who brought up our Lord Jesus from the dead, that great Shepherd of the sheep, through the *blood* of the everlasting covenant" (13.20).

These are the very themes we find in the Book of Revelation, which speaks of "Jesus Christ, the faithful witness," who loved us and washed us from our sins in his own *blood* (1.5). He is "worthy ... to open the seals" on the scroll of history, we tell him, "because you were slain, and have redeemed us to God by your *blood*" (5.9). Those who pass through the great tribulation are those who "washed their robes and made them white in the *blood* of the Lamb. Therefore they are before the throne of God, and serve him day and night in his temple. And he who sits upon the throne will dwell among them" (7.14–15). These are the believers, who are said to "overcome [the devil] by the *blood* of the Lamb" (12.11).

COMMENTARY

Chapter 1

Revelation 1.1–8

From the start this most interesting book describes itself as a written prophecy (verse 3; cf. 19.10; 22.7, 10, 18, 19).

In the early Church prophetic utterance played a major role in the determination of practical matters, such as the proper direction to be taken by missionaries (Acts 16.6–7) and the choice of men to be ordained (1 Tim 4.14). Indeed, the prophets in the New Testament are mentioned with the apostles (1 Cor 12.27–29; 14.1–5; Eph 2.20), and we even know the names of some of them (Acts 11.27–30; 15.32). The present book contains seven references to these prophets (10.7; 11.8; 16.6; 18.20–24; 22.6,9).

The author is John the Apostle, identical to the author of the Fourth Gospel and three New Testament epistles. If the John identified here was *not* that man, this enigmatic book would never have been included in the apostolic canon. The Church Fathers who determined these matters were *very* strict on the point.

The book itself is addressed to seven particular churches found in Asia Minor. It contains visions, that is, "all things that he saw," an expression found fifty-four times in this book. Nonetheless, Revelation begins like an epistle, "grace to you and peace," exactly like the epistles of Paul.

Revelation 1.9–20

John's vision comes "on the Lord's Day" (verse 10), Sunday (1 Cor 16.2), the very day when the seven churches of Asia Minor were celebrating the Lord's Supper, "the breaking of the Bread." This service of worship normally began on the night when the Sabbath came to a close and Sunday began; it lasted through the night and ended on Sunday morning (Acts 20.7, 11).

John describes himself as being "in the Spirit," a technical term referring to prophetic inspiration (Num 11.25; 2 Sam 23.2; Ez 2.2; 3.24; Mt 22.43). Like Ezekiel, John "fell as one dead" (verse 17), a description of the biblical phenomenon known as being "slain in the Spirit." Such was John's response to this inaugural vision (comparable to the inaugural visions of Isaiah and Ezekiel) of Christ in glory, standing in the midst of the Menorah (verse 12), clothed as the High Priest (verse 13; Ex 28.4; 39.29; Sir 50.5–12). The versatile "right hand" of the Lord can simultaneously hold the Pleiades (verse 16) and still be laid gently on the downfallen John (verse 17).

In this vision Christ is otherwise frightening, with his white hair (verse 14; Dan 7.9), the sword of the Word issuing from his mouth (verse 16; cf. 2.12, 16; 19.15; Eph 6.17; Heb 4.12), his feet like refined brass (verse 15; Ez 1.7). Here he is twice called "the First and the Last" (verses 11,17), an expression that will also appear in 2.8 and 22.13. Drawn from the Book of Isaiah (41.44; 44.6), this expression corresponds to "Alpha and Omega" (verses 8,11), the first and final letters of the Greek alphabet. Christ is, then, the beginning and end of language, the defining content of all intelligible meaning. He is, in short, the Word. He died and rose again and lives forever (verse 18; Rom 6.9). Hence, he holds the keys of death and the underworld (verse 18; cf. 9.1; 20.1).

Chapter 2

Revelation 2.1–7

Among the early Christian churches, Ephesus was particularly renowned for the strictness of its doctrinal purity. This was a book-burning congregation (Acts 19.19), which brooked no heresy. The apostle Paul, who had labored at Ephesus for three years, stressed the importance of doctrinal orthodoxy to all who ministered and taught there (Acts 20.29–31; 1 Tim 1.3–7,18–20; 4.1–3; 5.17; 6.3–5,20; 2 Tim 1.13–15; 2.14–18; 3.13; 4.2–5). In contrast to all of Paul's other epistles, he mentioned no heresies in his Epistle to the Ephesians. Well into the second century, we know the reputation of the church at Ephesus for its doctrinal purity (cf. Ignatius of Antioch, *Ephesians* 6.2; 9.1; Irenaeus of Lyons, *Against the Heresies* 1.26.3).

Here in Revelation 2 the church at Ephesus is commended for dealing with certain heretics called the Nicolaitans (verse 6), who apparently taught sexual immorality (2.14–15). The church was also obliged to deal with false apostles (verse 2), concerning whom the apostle Paul had earlier given warning to the elders of Ephesus (Acts 20.29; cf. 2 Cor 11.13–15; *Didache* 11).

The problem at Ephesus, then, was not a lack of orthodoxy, but a lack of charity; they had forgotten their first love (ἀγάπην—verse 4). At one time they had known fervent love (Acts 20.36–38), but now it had grown cold. John's words to them here stand forever as a warning to those whose zeal for doctrinal purity obscures in their minds the need for true charity. Even though the Ephesian Christians are here commended for their "works," labor," and "patience" (verse 2; cf. exactly these three words in 1 Thess 1.3), they have somehow fallen away from their "first works" (verse 5), as they have from their "first love."

The paradisiacal imagery of verse 7 comes from Genesis, of course, and will appear again in the final chapter of Revelation. The first of these seven letters to the Asian churches, then, makes it clear that the most serious dangers facing those churches did not come from external threat and persecution, but from spiritual problems within.

Revelation 2.8–11

Smyrna, the modern Turkish city of Izmir, was a seaport rivaling and then surpassing Ephesus. The Book of Revelation is our earliest historical witness to the presence of a Christian church at Smyrna, but it does not indicate when or by whom the place was evangelized.

A second century bishop of that church, the martyr Polycarp, one of the most revered men in early Christian history, personally knew the apostle John at one end of his ministry, and, at the other end, was the friend of Irenaeus of Lyons in Gaul, who lived to the dawn of the third century. Polycarp thus became the very embodiment of primitive Christian tradition, and because of him Smyrna's status among the early churches rivaled that of Ephesus.

At Smyrna there seems to have been considerable conflict between the Christians and the local Jews, who are here referred to as "a synagogue of Satan," not even worthy to be called real Jews (verse 9). Even in the mid-second century the Jews of Smyrna took steps to prevent the Christians from recovering the body of the martyred Polycarp.[1]

The four verses here under consideration indicate that, unlike the situations in Ephesus, Pergamum, Thyatira, Sardis, and Laodicea, in Smyrna the problems faced by the church came largely from without. Thus, unlike the Ephesians (2.5), the believers at Smyrna were not told to repent. John did warn the congregation, however,

---

[1] *The Martyrdom of Polycarp* 18.1.

that they would soon be severely tested (verse 10). How many Christians perished in that testing? It is very difficult to say, but we do know that Polycarp, who was martyred in AD 155, was the twelfth name on the list of martyrs at Smyrna.[2]

Those martyrs, in any case, were promised the "crown of life," an athletic image indicating their victory in Christ (Phil 3.14; 2 Tim 2.5; Jas 1.12; 1 Pet 5.4). The "second death" in verse 11 refers to eternal damnation (cf. 20.6, 14–15; 21.8).

Revelation 2.12–17

Pergamum is now the Turkish city of Bergama, which is about one-tenth the size it was in antiquity; it has had an unbroken history since the fifth century BC. There is a still a small, poor congregation of Christians at Bergama, the direct descendents of that congregation to which the Book of Revelation was addressed. One may also see there the ruins of a once magnificent church dedicated to St John by the Emperor Theodosius in the fourth century. Thanks to the excavations begun under the auspices of the Museum of Berlin in 1878, we know quite a bit about the ancient city.

The problems in the church at Pergamum seem to have been largely internal. There was a laxist group, apparently to be identified with the Nicolaitans (verse 15), who advocated sexual immorality and the eating of sacrifices made to idols (verse 14). Those internal problems were compounded, nonetheless, by external pressure in the form of occasional persecutions, during one of which the martyr Antipas perished (verse 13), who is identified by Christian tradition as the first bishop of that city (with an annual feast day on April 11).

So resolute was the opposition to the gospel in Pergamum that Satan was said to be enthroned there, perhaps a reference to the temple of the god Asculepius, whose symbol was a staff with a coiled serpent. That image, now universally known as the symbol of the healing professions (Asculepius was the god of healing), would have

---

[2] *The Martyrdom of Polycarp* 19.1.

reminded the early Christians of the serpent in Genesis 3, which will reappear several more times in the Book of Revelation (cf. 12.9 and 20.2, for instance). Pergamum also boasted temples to Zeus and to Roma, the deified personification of the empire. In verse 16 Jesus says that he will come quickly, a promise repeated six more times in Revelation (3.11; 16.15; 22.7, 12, 17, 20).

Revelation 2.18–29

Thyatira, the modern Akhisar, was a city more modest than the previous three. The church in that city, too, was praised for its works, love, service, faith, and patience (verse 19).

In spite of that praise, the congregation tolerated the activities of a pseudo-charismatic woman in its midst whom John likened to the ancient Queen Jezebel of Israel, that fine Phoenician feminist responsible for so many of the ills condemned by the prophet Elijah in the ninth century BC (verse 20). The moral offenses of the woman at Thyatira, which included the advocacy of sexual sins and the eating of food sacrificed to demons, seem similar to those of the Nicolaitans, but in the present case John took care to single out an individual rather than to talk about a group. Against her he prophesied a dire judgment (verses 22–23). This woman seems also to have been a sort of mistress of the occult, here called "the depths of Satan" (verse 24).

But John does not solely condemn that woman; he speaks very critically, in addition, of the church that tolerated her activities (verse 20). Toleration, which today is everywhere regarded as a virtue to be cultivated, is everywhere in the New Testament regarded as a vice to be avoided (for example, Rom 1.32).

In the instance studied here, the church at Thyatira was permitting a very forceful woman, who claimed the authority of a prophetess, to bring moral havoc into the congregation. Whereas the members of the congregation were intimidated by her influence, or were simply reluctant to deal harshly with a woman, John, as we see, suffered from neither that intimidation nor that reluctance. In the present text he accomplished the moral equivalent of that robust defenestration suffered by the aging Phoenician princess of Samaria on that judgment day when Jehu came a-riding (2 Kgs 9.30–37).

Chapter 3

Revelation 3.1–6

In antiquity Sardis had been the capital city of the famous Croesus, king of Lydia, and in Persian times it was the greatest city of Asia Minor, linked by a major highway to the faraway Persian capital of Susa. The acropolis of the city was so high and well fortified as to be nearly impregnable. In fact, it was never taken by direct assault. It was captured twice, however, on both occasions by sneak attacks, once by Cyrus in 546 and once by Antiochus the Great in 218.

It is against another surprise attack that John warns the people of Sardis now (verse 3), using an image found elsewhere in the New Testament (Mt 24.43; 1 Thess 5.2; 2 Pet 3.10). Truth to tell, lack of vigilance was a great problem in the church at Sardis, part of its more general condition of laziness and despondency. After all, John does not mention a single heresy at Sardis. The evil in that congregation is, rather, apathy and boredom; the congregation is too dead to be sick (verse 1).

Therefore, John summons them to vigilance (verse 2). Very few Christians in Sardis have measured up (verse 4), and the others are in danger of being removed from "the Book of Life" (verse 5; cf. also 17.8; 21.27). This latter image is not a metaphor for eternal predestination, obviously, precisely because names *can be* removed from it.

The Book of Life is, rather, a register of the citizens of heaven, and the metaphor of erasure testifies that the names written therein, as long as those who bear those names still live on earth, can be removed if the removal is warranted. There is no question, then, of some sort of eternal roll call already fixed and unchangeable, independent of the choices each man makes in his own heart. As long as he is on this earth, there remains the possibility that a man's name may be erased from the Book of Life. Hence, the necessity of vigilance.

Revelation 3.7–13

This is the most cheerful, complimentary, and optimistic of the letters to the seven Asian churches. Not one word of criticism is directed to the Christians at Philadelphia. On the contrary, they are twice praised for their perseverance (verses 8, 10). The problem at Philadelphia is external, involving conflict with the local Jews (verse 9), the sort of problem we saw at Smyrna.

"The key of David" (verse 7) alludes to Isaiah 22.22, where Eliakim is described as having exclusive power of the keys. A minister with this power was the man who decided who would and who would not be admitted to the royal presence. In describing Jesus in this way, John asserts that if anyone wants to go to God, he must go through Jesus. This emphasis on the unique mediation and finality of Christ is common throughout the New Testament.

The Christian congregation at Philadelphia is evidently small and of limited resources, but we get the impression that it is about to make significant missionary gains ("open door"; see Acts 14.27; 1 Cor 16.9; 2 Cor 2.12; Col 4.3). Also, there will soon be a trial (verse 10), and those who overcome in that trial will receive the name of God and the name of New Jerusalem (verse 12), the holy city that comes down from heaven (21.2; Gal 2.9).

St Paul contrasts the *new* Jerusalem with the *now* Jerusalem (τῇ νῦν Ἰερουσαλήμ), which is simply a city in Palestine (Gal 4.24–25). By the time that John writes, this latter city, the earthly Jerusalem, has already been destroyed by the Romans.

Revelation 3.14–22

We commented, with respect to the church at Philadelphia, that John had no criticisms to make about that congregation. Writing to

Ephesus, Smyrna, Pegamos, Thyatira, and Sardis, John paid some compliments and made some criticisms. Writing to the Christians at Laodicea, however, John has nothing at all encouraging to say! He is unable to find a single item for which to praise that church. To John's thinking, the church at Laodicea is a lackluster group of slackers living in an affluent, self-satisfied society. Although this church was evangelized by Paul's companion Epaphras (Col 4.12–13), it has lost its fervor and is now mediocre (verse 16).

The secular city of Laodicea was famous for three things: (1) its large banking interests, (2) its textile industry, and (3) a special eye-salve that the great physician Galen called "Phrygian powder." John alludes to all three things in verse 18, where the church at Laodicea is told to come to God for (1) gold refined in the fire, (2) clothing to cover its nakedness, and (3) a special anointing of its spiritual eyes. The Laodiceans must admit, in short, that they are "poor, blind, and naked" (verse 17).

There are three points of Christology to note in this letter to Laodicea: (1) Christ in the past: the relationship of Christ to creation (verse 14; cf. Col 1.15–18; Heb 1.1–3; Jn 1.3); (2) Christ in the present: exhorting and inviting his Church, communing with those who open to him (verses 19–20; cf. 19.9; Lk 22.28–30); (3) Christ in the future: rewarding those who vanquish in his name (verse 21; cf. Mt 19.28). The image of the divine throne appears over forty times in the Book of Revelation. The present mention of it prepares for John's vision in the following chapter.

Chapter 4

Revelation 4.1–11

In Chapters 2 and 3 John has warned the Christians of the seven churches of Asia that judgment is imminent. He has endeavored to strengthen them for an impending outbreak of chaos and disorder.

In the present chapter, John turns their vision on high, to the throne of God, which is the source of all order. Like Amos, Isaiah, Micah, and other prophets, John slips into an ecstatic trance, a rapture in which he is seized by the Holy Spirit. He hears a voice, and a mysterious door opens (verse 1). He is introduced to the heavenly worship before God's throne (verse 2), over which is the rainbow of the covenant (verse 3; Gen 9.12–17). The dominant color is green, the symbol of spring and hope.

As in the temple of Solomon (1 Kgs 7.23), which was modeled, after all, on the heavenly throne room, there is "a sea of glass, like crystal" (verse 6), symbolizing the chaos over which the Holy Spirit brooded in Creation. Other details remind us of Isaiah 6 and Ezekiel 1. This should not surprise us, because in all of Holy Scripture we are dealing with the same God and the same heaven. The hymn, with which the chapter closes, concentrates on creation. Recall that this vision takes place on Sunday (1.10), the first day of creation.

Chapter 5

Revelation 5.1–7

Because the earliest Christians were Jews, their experience of worship was tightly tied to the style of the synagogue. In the weekly worship at the synagogue, a special liturgical moment came when a reader took the sacred scroll of God's word, opened it, read it to the congregation, and then explained it.

For Christians, this solemn rite held a particular significance, because they believed that the words of the sacred scroll were completed and fulfilled by Jesus the Messiah. Thus, the opening, reading, and interpretation of the sacred scroll was perceived as a symbol of what Jesus accomplished in his ministry, death, and resurrection.

There is a story bearing this symbolism in Luke 4.16–21, where Jesus himself took, read, and interpreted God's word in the synagogue at Nazareth, finishing by referring the entire text to himself. That Lukan passage at the beginning of Jesus' earthly ministry forms a literary inclusion with the action of Jesus at the end of Luke, where the wounded Lord ("Behold my hands and my feet, that it is I myself") explains the meaning of Holy Scripture to the Church by referring it to his own ministry, death, and resurrection (24.25–27, 32).

That is to say, the Church believes that the ministry, death, and resurrection of Christ the Lord have an exegetical quality; it is interpretation in act. This primitive conviction of the Christian faith that only Jesus can "open the scroll" is at the heart of what John now sees in the throne room of heaven (verse 7). The Lamb of God, who takes away the sins of the world, can open this Scroll precisely because he died and rose again (verse 9). This Lamb "stands" before

God, standing being the proper posture of a priest (cf. Acts 7.55–56; Heb 10.11).

Although the image of Christ as the Lamb is common in the New Testament (Jn 1.29,36; 19.36; Acts 8.32; 1 Cor 5.7; 1 Pet 1.18–19), it is utterly dominant in the Book of Revelation, where it appears twenty-eight times. The Lamb in Revelation 5 stands in his immolated, mactated state, "as though slain," still bearing in his flesh the wounds of his passion (cf. Jn 20.25, 27). This picture of Jesus as the wound-bearing Lamb, opening the Scriptures, is strikingly parallel to that of the risen Lord at the end of Luke's Gospel (Lk 24.38–46).

Revelation 5.8–14

In this scene "the twenty-four elders fell down before the Lamb" (verse 8) in the posture of adoration. This is the posture that we commonly find people assuming in the presence of Jesus in the gospel stories, but more especially in the Gospel according to Matthew (cf. 2.2, 8, 11; 8.2; 9.18; 14.33; 15.25; 20.20; 28.9). Jesus is adored as equal to the Father.

Likewise, two of the three short hymns in this chapter are addressed to Christ. The first is called a "new song," an expression derived from the Book of Psalms and Isaiah 42.10–13. It is a "new song," not in the sense of the "latest hit," but because it comes from and gives expression to the definitive newness of life given us in redemption. The new song is of a piece with our new name, the new heaven, and the new earth. This is the eternal newness purchased by the blood of Christ (verse 9), who makes us kings and priests (verse 10; cf. 1.5–6; 1 Pet 2.5, 9; Ex 19.6).

He has drawn us "out of (ἐκ) every tribe and tongue and people and nation"; this idea, which appears repeatedly in Revelation (7.9; 10.11; 11.9; 13.7; 14.6; 17.15), is largely inspired by the Book of Daniel (3.4, 7; 5.19; 6.25).

In verse 11 the whole choir of heaven joins in the "new song" of the twenty-four elders who ascribe seven things to the Lamb (verse

12), and in verse 13 the whole of creation follows suit. This hymn extends the praise of God in Chapter 4 and joins the Lamb to that praise, in which heaven and earth are united in a common worship. To understand the significance of this common worship, we should bear in mind that the context of these visions is the Church at worship in the Sunday Eucharist (cf. 1.10). These hymns in Chapters 4 and 5 were surely sung by the Church on earth as well as the Church in heaven.

Chapter 6

Revelation 6.1–8

The opening of the first four seals brings forth four horses, variously colored in a way reminiscent of Zechariah 1.8–11; 6.1–7, though in Revelation the attention is directed more to the riders than to the horses.

The first, the mounted archer on the white horse, symbolizes invasion and war. The mounted archers contemporary with John were the Parthian warriors to the eastern border of the Roman Empire (verses 1–2), on the far side of the Euphrates (cf. 9.14; 16.12).

The second rider, which is like unto it, rides a red horse, which symbolizes bloodshed and fire. Whereas the first horseman carried a bow, the second carries a sword (verse 4). War invariably leads to famine and starvation, symbolized in the third horse, a black one, whose rider carries scales to measure the scant remaining food (verses 5–6).

Green, the color of the fourth horse, is the color of white human flesh at the beginnings of decay. The rider of this horse, therefore, is named Death, which perhaps is a metaphor for plague (verse 8), as in the common expression "Black Death" to mean bubonic plague. With war, famine, and disease, the populace is dying too fast to be buried; their rotting corpses are left for the beasts of the field. For this combination of evils, compare our text to Luke 21.9–11.

These afflictions were visited on the world that John knew. In AD 62 the Roman legions were defeated by the Parthians to the east,[3] and there were shortages of food, such as those recorded in the Acts of

---

[3] Cf. Tacitus, *Annals* 15.13–17.

the Apostles and in Suetonius.[4] In addition, there were earthquakes, such as those in Asia Minor itself in AD 60,[5] volcanic eruptions, such as Vesuvius,[6] civil war in Rome following the suicide of Nero in 68, and the war in Judea that culminated in the destruction of Jerusalem in AD 70. All these events, John is telling us, were the subjects of the sacred scroll opened by the Lamb. That is to say, they are all the fulfillment of prophecies in the final times.

Revelation 6.9–17

Besides the evils that afflict the people of the world, John knows of a special harm visited on Christians. After his description of the four horsemen, therefore, he speaks of the bloody persecution endured by believers (verses 9–11). Their blood (in the biblical idiom, their "souls," because the soul is in the blood, according to Leviticus 17.11) has run down the side of the altar of sacrifice and pools at its base. They are martyrs, which is the Greek word for "witnesses." Like the blood of Abel, their blood cries out to God, "How long?" (cf. Is 6.11; Zech 1.12; Hab 1.2; Dan 8.13; 12.6).

The vengeance for which they pray is not a personal vindictiveness (for Christians always forgive their enemies and wish them no harm; this is an absolute rule, allowing no exceptions), but a petition for the fulfilling of God's righteous historical purposes.

They must wait, however, until the full measure of the martyrs is complete (cf. Heb 11.40). Their white robes signify their participation in eternal life (cf. Rev 7.13–17). The opening of the sixth seal declares those things that precede the end of the world and the final vindication of the saints.

First come the perturbations of the earth (verses 12–14), and then the effects on human beings (verses 15–17). The sequence of these afflictions follows the order of creation in Genesis 1: namely, (1) earth, (2) sun, (3) moon, (4) stars, (5) firmament, (6) land, (7) man.

[4]Ibid. 14.27.
[5]Seutonius, *The Lives of the Caesars,* "Domitian" 7.
[6]Pliny, *Letters* 6.16.

What John sees, then, is a kind of de-creation, a reversal of what God established, the collapse of the universe.

In the opening of the fifth, sixth, and seventh seals, we also detect the same four colors that accompanied the first four seals. thus, fifth seal, white robes; sixth seal, red moon and black sun; seventh seal, green grass.

There is a great irony in the image of the "wrath of the Lamb." Indeed, a wrathful lamb is unimaginable except to the enemies of God. The wrath, of course, does not come from the Lamb who shed his blood for the world's redemption and who hates nothing that he has made. The wrath comes, rather, from within the enemies themselves, who insist on seeing God as an enemy.

Chapter 7

Revelation 7.1–8

The two visions in this chapter still pertain to the sixth seal. The opening of the first six seals has unleashed enormous sufferings on the earth, so prior to the opening of the seventh the vision of St John faces the question, "Who shall stand? Who will be able to endure? Who will persevere to the end?" And John's answer is, "the servants of God."

Prior to the releasing of the final tribulation, therefore, the servants of God must be sealed. Their number, 144,000, is a massive combination of the perfect number twelve (3 x 4, or the divine number 3 multiplied by the human number 4; that is to say, the multiplied combination of God and man) multiplied to a gross and then multiplied again by a thousand. That is to say, a very big number that no man can count (verse 9; cf. Gen 15.5).

The final preservation of God's elect was foreshadowed in their deliverance at the time of the fall of Jerusalem in AD 70. Because of a prophecy that told them all to flee,[7] no Christians were in Jerusalem when the city came under siege. Although up to a million Jews perished during the horrors of that siege and downfall, not one of them was a Christian. The physical deliverance of those Christians thus became the symbol of the spiritual deliverance of God's elect in the final tribulation. (And this latter deliverance is spiritual, not physical. There is no suggestion in the Book of Revelation that believers will be "raptured" away and spared the sufferings of the rest of the earth. Indeed, Revelation has a great deal to say about the sufferings of Christians during the final times.)

[7]Cf. Eusebius, *Ecclesiastical History* 3.5.3.

In order to be spiritually spared, they must be sealed. This sealing of God's servants is done with the mark of the "tau," the last letter of the Hebrew alphabet (Ez 9.1–7), which at that time was still cruciform. That is to say, God's servants are sealed with the sign of the cross on their foreheads, which in fact was a very early part of the rite of baptism.[8] To be thus sealed was a sign that Christians belonged to God (cf. Is 44.5; 2 Cor 1.22; Gal 6.17; Eph 1.13; 4.30; Jn 6.27).

This sealing with the mark of the true Paschal Lamb fulfilled the promise contained in that earlier marking of Israel with the sacrificial blood of its type (Ex 12.21–23). Both Ezekiel and Exodus are important for the understanding of this seal. Ezekiel's reference was to the fall of Jerusalem in 587 BC, of which everyone was aware who saw the fall of Jerusalem in AD 70. The passage in Exodus 12 had to do with the last of the ten plagues visited upon Egypt, the slaying of the firstborn sons. This sealing in Revelation, then, involves a new Exodus, in which God's people will be delivered, not left to share in the sin of the earthly Jerusalem.

Revelation 7.9–17

Beginning with an "amen" by which they respond to the acclamation of the saints in verse 10, the angels now join their voices in the praise of God (verse 11).

In John's perspective, this vision is simultaneously past, present, and future. Inasmuch as the vision already contains fulfillment, its verbal tense is past. The "great tribulation," moreover, has already started (for it is simultaneous with the "last times"), and therefore the present verbal tense, the ongoing perspective, is likewise proper. But inasmuch as there are still events to come (quickly!), John's view is also directed toward the future.

One of the elders clarifies for the seer the identity of those clad in white robes (6.11; 7.9). They have already passed through the great tribulation, he tells John (verse 14; cf. Dan 12.1; Mk 13.19), a

[8]Cf. Tertullian, *Against Marcion* 3.22.

description suggesting that the great tribulation, at least from their perspective, is already past. Yet, that tribulation itself will not be narrated until 13.7–10.

They are called "martyrs," but this designation should be interpreted in a broader theological perspective that regards the call to martyrdom as implicit in the very nature of baptism. Indeed, from earliest times the white robe has been associated with baptism, that rite by which believers are washed in the blood of the Lamb. Christians do not receive their white robes in heaven; on the contrary, they will not even be admitted to heaven unless they are already wearing those white robes (22.14). To wear the white robe means to live "in the blood" (Rom 3.25; 5.9; 1 Cor 11.25; Eph 1.7; 2.13; Col 1.20; Heb 9.14; 1 Pet 1.2,19; 1 Jn 1.7).

The true servants of God, moreover, are engaged in his unceasing worship (verse 15; 21.5; 22.5); thus, they share already in the life of heaven. In the final two verses of this chapter the verbs return to the future tense, indicating that an unfulfilled history still remains, through which God's servants must pass. The image also shifts from the Lamb to the Shepherd, both images being essential to a complete Christology.

Chapter 8

Revelation 8.1–13

The number four is the traditional human number; thus, man divides his world into four directions: a front, a back, and two sides. He speaks of "four winds," the "four corners of the earth," and so forth. The divine number is three, because it is perceived to be the most stable. The triangle is the only stable geometric figure, the angles of which cannot be altered without changing the length of its sides. Similarly, the tripod is the only completely stable object to stand on a plane; anyone sitting on a wobbly chair knows that chairs seem to prefer three legs to four!

Any combination of three and four, therefore, represents the union of God and man, which is perfection. Thus, the multiplication of three and four yields the sacred number twelve, which appears in many contexts in Holy Scripture, including the Book of Revelation. If three and four are added, the resultant sacred number is seven. The symbolic use of both numbers, twelve and seven (one being the number of months in the year, and the other being the number of days in the week), is found ubiquitously in Holy Scripture.

The number seven, in fact, provides an important structural element throughout much of Revelation. Thus, there were seven letters to seven churches (Chapters 2 and 3), followed by a scroll with seven seals that needed to be opened. The opening of that seventh seal, in turn, will introduce the seven trumpets, which will be followed by seven bowls of plagues.

In the present text, the immediate response to the opening of the seventh seal is silence in heaven for thirty minutes (verse 1), while the angels with the seven trumpets prepare themselves (verses 2, 6), and the throne room is ritually incensed (verse 3). The silence that accompanies the incensing provides a time for prayers to be offered, the ascending of which is symbolized in the rising incense smoke (cf. Lk 1.9–10; Ex 30.1–9; *Talmud*, "Tamid" 3.1). In the temple ritual of Israel, it is likely that thirty minutes was required for the priest to make the rounds of the temple with his censer, though it sometimes took longer (cf. Lk 1.21).

We should also observe here that the altar of incense is the only altar in heaven (6.9; 9.13; 14.18; 16.7); there is no altar of holocausts in heaven because the purpose of that altar in Israel's ancient temple was fulfilled by the cross, where the definitive sacrifice was offered for the sins of the world.

The trumpets, moreover, will be sounded by the seven "angels of the presence" (cf. Tob 12.15; Lk 1.19). The trumpets themselves are best understood in two points of reference. First, there were seven trumpets sounded in the procession around the walls of Jericho in Joshua 6. It is useful to bear in mind that the Ark of the Covenant was borne at the end of that procession, after the seven trumpets. Similarly, at the end of the sounding of the seventh trumpet in the Book of Revelation, the Ark of the Covenant will once again appear (cf. 11.15, 19).

Second, that event of the fall of Jericho was given a constant liturgical expression in the ritual of the Jerusalem temple by the sounding of the trumpets (1 Chron 15.24; Neh 12.4–42). Almost any time anything of significance happened in the worship at the temple, such as prayers, sacrifices, and so forth, the trumpets were sounded. Thus, the blare of the trumpet symbolized Israel's constant and sustained worship of God. This is also the function of the trumpets here in Revelation 8.

The blowing of the seven trumpets parallels the opening of the seven seals in several close particulars. Thus, the first four trumpets form a unified whole (verses 7–12), as did the first four seals (6.1–8). As in the case of the fifth and sixth seals (6.9–17), the fifth and sixth trumpets will be expressed in a longer and separate narrative

(9.1–21). Finally, a pair of visions will precede the sounding of the seventh trumpet (10.1–11.14), as another pair preceded the opening of the seventh seal (7.1–17).

In addition, by introducing various plagues upon the earth, the seven trumpets find another extensive parallel in the seven bowls of plague that will follow them. Finally, let us note that the plagues visited on the earth at the sounding of the trumpets, like the plagues visited on Egypt, do not touch those who, having been sealed, belong to God.

Chapter 9

The first four trumpets produced plagues that resembled the seventh, first, and ninth plagues of Egypt (Ex 9.22–26; 7.20–21; 10.21). These plagues, prompted by the trumpets, affect only the physical and astrophysical world, not human beings—at least not directly. The final three, described by the heavenly eagle as "woes," afflict mankind directly (8.13).

The image of a fallen star already appeared in 8.10–11. Now another star falls in response to the fifth trumpet (verse 1; cf. Is 14.12–20). This star opens the bottomless pit, from which arises a hellish smoke (verse 2; cf. 8.12) that contrasts with the incense smoke of prayer. The abyss represents existence without the worship of God—the theological term for which is "hell." As John watches, a massive swarm of locusts takes form within that hellish cloud (verse 3), reminiscent of Egypt's eighth plague (Ex 10.12–15). Unlike those former locusts, however, these locusts attack men themselves, not plant life (verse 4). Their activity is limited to five months, which is roughly the normal life span of locusts.

Indeed, this may be the only feature in which these particular locusts in Revelation resemble any other locusts in the world. These are not your usual, run-of-the-mill locusts (verses 8–10). They are satanic locusts, denizens of the abyss, who afflict men with despair. They deceptively have human faces (verse 7), but they represent a worse than human evil. Their king is called "Abaddon" (Ἀβαδδών, a transliteration of אֲבַדּוֹן) which is the Old Testament's personification of the underworld, or grave. It literally means "destruction" (cf.

Job 26.6; 31.12). John translates this name into Greek as Ἀπολλύων, meaning "destroyer" (verse 11).

It is possible that John intends here a word play on the name "Apollo," which name, according to Aeschylus, comes from the verb ἀπολύειν, "to destroy."[9] We may bear in mind, in this respect, that the Emperor Domitian, not a man easily outdone, it must be said, with respect to a high self-opinion, proclaimed himself a manifestation of Apollo. (There is simply no evil as evil as official, government-sanctioned evil.) The torture inflicted by these followers of Abaddon is spiritual, not physical, and the Christians, sealed with the sign of the living God, are exempt from it.

Revelation 9.13–21

To the citizens of the Roman Empire the Euphrates River was a symbol analogous to the "Iron Curtain" of the Cold War era, that is, a border beyond which the enemy world lay massively in menace (verse 14). The enemy in their case was the Parthian army, whose most memorable feature was its cavalry of archers. Guiding their mounts with their knees, and thus leaving both hands free, those fearsome Parthian horsemen could shoot arrows very quickly in all directions, including to the rear. This is perhaps the point of reference for John's image of horses that bite with both their mouths and their tails (verse 19). By such means, says John, God will further chastise those who persecute his people.

Many details of this vision evoked by the sixth trumpet have striking parallels in Ezekiel 38–39. Fierce as it was, however, the Parthian army was never as fearsome as that described by John (verses 17–18). This is the army of hell, whose immense reserves are superior to all merely human forces. The number given by John, "two hundred million" (verse 16), would certainly constitute the largest army ever assembled. To gain something of its magnitude, we may

[9]Aeschylus, *Agamemnon* 1082.

bear in mind that Alexander the Great captured everything from the Danube to the Indus with an army of a hundred thousand.

The army that John sees, like the army of locusts summoned by the previous trumpet, comes right out of hell. Both of these invaders, the locusts and the horsemen, are sent to encourage men to repentance, but men's hearts, like the heart of Pharaoh, are hardened. The idolatries listed in verse 20 are the root of the other moral evils listed in verse 21. This relationship of idolatry to moral evil is identical to that in Romans 1.21–32 and Ephesians 5.6.

Chapter 10

Revelation 10.1–11

Just as there was a double interrupting narrative immediately prior to the opening of the seventh seal, so a pair of visions will now precede the sounding of the seventh trumpet: the angel holding the little scroll, and the two faithful witnesses.

In the first of these, John is struck by the angel's numinous character, at once bright and obscure. The angel's body is clothed in a cloud, reminiscent of the cloud of the divine presence during ancient Israel's desert journey and the cloud associated with the tabernacle of the divine presence. The face of the angel, on the other hand, has the luminosity of the sun. Nonetheless, the very fierceness of his countenance is tempered by the rainbow arching over his head, a reminder of the eternal covenant between God and creation in Genesis 9. The angel's legs are pillars of fire, an image also reminiscent of the Exodus. His voice is like the roaring of a lion (verse 3), which is echoed by the seven thunders from Psalm 29 (28).

With one foot on the earth, one foot on the sea, and his hand into the air, the angel touches, as it were, all three aspects of physical creation: solid, liquid, and gas (verse 5). Moreover, all three of these components are mentioned in his oath (verse 6; Ex 20.4, 11), in which he swears that the fulfillment of God's secret purpose (τὸ μυστήριον) in history will not be delayed.

The scroll the angel holds is smaller than the scroll in Chapter 5, a detail suggesting that its message may be less universal. Indeed, the message of that scroll is not directed to the world, but to the community of faith (verses 8–11). It is not read but eaten; John absorbs its message into himself. He assimilates the Word that he might then give expression to it. In this respect he imitates the prophet Ezekiel (cf. Ez 2.9–3.4).

Chapter 11

Revelation 11.1–10

In our reading of the Book of Revelation thus far we have encountered the Danielic expression, "a time, times, and half a time" (Dan 12.7). If we substitute the word "year" for "time," the meaning of the expression is clear: "three and a half years," or forty-two months, or (following the Hebrew calendar of thirty days per month) twelve-hundred and sixty days. In the Book of Daniel this was the length of time during which the Jerusalem temple was violated by Antiochus Epiphanes IV (Dan 9.27).

Similarly here in Revelation it is the symbolic length of time of severe trial and the apparent triumph of evil (verses 2–3; 12.6; 13.5). John's contemporaries must also have been struck by the fact that the Roman siege of Jerusalem also lasted three and a half years, from AD 67–70. In the present chapter this length of time refers to the persecution of the Christian Church, of which Jerusalem's temple was a type and foreshadowing.

Within the Christian Church, however, we find an inner court, as it were, a deep interior dimension that the forces of evil cannot trample. This inviolability is conferred by being sealed with the sign of the living God. It asserts that believers are not to fear those who can kill the body but can do no more (cf. Mt 10.28), because there yet remains an inner court that is off-limits to the invader and defiler. This is the inner court of which John is told to take the measure (cf. Ez 40.1–4; Zech 2.1–2), a measuring that he will narrate later (21.15–17).

The literary background of John's vision of the two witnesses is Zechariah 4.1–3, 11–14, where the prophet has in mind the anointed

ruler Zerubbabel and the anointed priest Jeshua, the two men who
preserved the worship in God's house. Those two figures represented
royalty (Zerubbabel was a descendent of David) and priesthood
(Jeshua was a descendent of Aaron), which are two essential aspects
of the life in Christ (cf. Rev 1.6; 5.10).

"Two" witnesses are required, of course, this being the minimum
number required in order "to make the case" (Deut 19.15). But the
two witnesses in this chapter of Revelation are the heirs, not only to
Zerubbabel and Jeshua, but also to Moses and Elijah. It was the first
of these who afflicted Egypt with plagues, and the second who closed
up heaven for three and a half years (cf. Lk 4.25; Jas 5.17). This is John's
way of asserting that the Christian Church, in her royal priesthood,
continues also the prophetic war against false gods. She will destroy
God's enemies by fire (verse 5), as did Moses (Num 16.35) and Elijah
(2 Kgs 1.9–12).

When the monster from the abyss kills these two servants of God
(verse 7), the forces of evil seem to have triumphed (verse 10), but
they will be carried up to heaven, again like Moses[10] and Elijah (2
Kgs 2.11), because the victorious Lamb has the final word.

Revelation 11.11–19

With respect to the prophets Moses and Elijah, whose outlines
appear in this vision as symbolic representations, we know that the
"return" of both men was expected by John's contemporaries (cf. Jn
1.21; Mk 6.15; 8.20). Both men did "return" at our Lord's transfiguration; indeed, in Mark 9 and Matthew 17, the question of the return
of Elijah is precisely the point of the conversation that immediately
follows the transfiguration.

When the two witnesses ascend into heaven (verse 12), one tenth
of the city falls (verse 13), the city in question still being "Sodom and
Egypt, where also our Lord was crucified" (verse 8). This one tenth
of the city, calculated as seven thousand souls, is literally a *tithe* of

---

[10]Josephus, *Antiquities* 4.8.48.

the city's population. Thus, the number of those who perish is a sort of direct reversal of the seven thousand who were saved in Elijah's remnant (1 Kgs 19.18).

Thus ends the second woe, which is the sixth trumpet (verse 14). The first six trumpets were warning blasts, whereas the seventh will be a kind of fanfare (verse 15).

In the hymn that follows the seventh trumpet (verses 17–18), we should especially observe that God's wrath is salvific, a matter at which believers will rejoice, because God's reign is established by his wrath. God is not a neutral observer of history. On the contrary, he is deeply biased on the side of the poor and oppressed. Some people in this world are poor and oppressed, because other people in this world worship false gods. In the biblical view, poverty and oppression are the results of idolatry, and this provokes God's wrath. His wrath is against the false gods and their servants, and believers are summoned to rejoice in the victory of that wrath, because it is the victory of freedom over slavery, justice over injustice, and Moses over Pharaoh. The wrath of God is the last thing in the world that Christians should be afraid of, for the wrath of God is on their side (Mt 23.35–36).

As in the ancient procession around Jericho, the Ark of the Covenant appears after the seventh trumpet (verse 19).

Chapter 12

Revelation 12.1–17

Though it is surely no myth, this awesome vision bears a more than slight resemblance to certain themes in ancient mythology. For example, there was the very primitive solar myth concerning the powers of darkness, which appear to triumph over the sun and to reign over the time of night, defying the promised sun. This darkness, which has usurped the reign of the sun, attempts to devour the sun in its very birth; to kill the sun, that is to say, as it emerges from its mother's womb.

In at least two versions of this ancient myth, in fact, the darkness is portrayed as a dragon-like snake. Thus, Egypt has its myth of the dragon Set, who pursued Isis while she carried the sun god Horus in her womb. Set's plan was to devour Horus at his birth. It is further curious that Isis, like the Woman in Revelation 12 (verse 14), is portrayed in Egyptian art (on an elaborate door in the King Tut collection, for instance) with wings, so that she could flee from Set.

Similarly, Greek mythology describes the dragon-snake Python as pursuing the goddess Leto, who is pregnant with the sun god Apollo. In both cases, the little child escapes and later returns to destroy the usurping serpent. The similarities of both of these myths to the vision in Revelation 12 are rather striking. Both myths also touch on the subject of the illegitimate "usurper," a theme Matthew develops in his story of Herod seeking to destroy the true King, Jesus, at his very birth.

John's vision takes place in the vault of heaven, where the Woman is described as a "sign," an image reminiscent of Isaiah 7.10–11. Indeed, John seems to be saying that in the birth of Jesus Isaiah's prophecy of virgin birth is fulfilled (cf. also Is 26.17). Like Christ himself (Rev 1.16), this Woman is clothed with the sun. All Christians know the virginity of the mother of Jesus. Is this Woman being represented, therefore, as the zodiacal sign of Virgo? It would seem so, because, like the sign for Virgo, there are twelve stars involved. In the southern hemisphere the six stars crowning Virgo are sigma, chi, iota, pi, nu, and beta. In the northern hemisphere they are theta, star 60, delta, star 93, second-magnitude beta, and omicron.

Nonetheless, this is not simply a description of the Lord's nativity. The Woman in the vision is the mother of Jesus, but she is more; she is also the Church, which gives birth to Christ in the world. The sufferings and persecution of the Church are described as birth pangs (cf. Jn 16.21–22).

The serpent, of course, is the ancient dragon that is the enemy of our race, the one who seduced the first woman in the garden. Now he must face the new Woman, who is more than a match for him. His seven heads put one in mind of the ancient mythological dragon Hydra, well known from a Canaanite narrative found in the excavations at Ras Shamra and from the traditional story of the Labors of Hercules. In Revelation it is clearly Satan, the Accuser (verse 10) from the Book of Job and from Zechariah 3.

Michael appears right out of the Book of Daniel, of course; in the New Testament he is spoken of only here and in the Epistle of Jude.

Chapter 13

Revelation 13.1–10

Up till now we have seen two beasts, one of them from the underworld (Chapter 11) and the other from the heavens (Chapters 12). Two more beasts will appear in the present chapter, one of them from the sea (verse 1), who also has seven heads and ten horns (cf. 12.3), and one from the land (verse 11).

The present reading is concerned solely with the first of these two latter beasts. Like the beast in Daniel 7, he is a composite of several menacing things (verse 2). He derives his "authority" from the Dragon (verses 2, 4) whom we considered in Chapter 12. That is to say, this beast shares in the power of Satan.

With respect to his ten horns, two remarks are in order. First, in Daniel 7, the obvious literary background here, the ten horns seem to refer to the ten Seleucid successors of Alexander the Great. Second, here in Revelation 13 they seem to refer to Roman emperors. If we leave out Otho, who reigned over the Roman Empire for only three months, there were, in fact, exactly ten Roman emperors up to Domitian, who was responsible for the persecution of AD 95. Augustus, Tiberius, Caligula, Claudius, Nero, Galba, Vitellius, Vespasian, Titus, and Domitian. Almost all of these men were recognized as divine, some of them even before their deaths. Words such as θεός and *divus* appear on their coins. This figure, therefore, symbolizes the idolatrous pretensions of the Roman Empire, which John ascribes to Satan. Those pretensions claim an unquestioned and absolute allegiance over the human spirit.

This beast of the Roman Empire combines the worst features of all the earlier empires. Daniel's winged lion of Babylon, the bear of the Medes, the leopard of the Persians, and the ten-headed hydra of the Greeks. One may note that John lists these components in the reverse order of Daniel.

Far more than ourselves, one fears, the early Christians were aware of the power of evil in the world. They spoke of it frequently in personified forms that are difficult to interpret literally. And the Christians described their relationship to this evil as one of warfare. The terms of the conflict described here in Revelation 13 may be compared to the description in 2 Thessalonians 2.3–12. In each case there is a widespread deception of people, their enslavement and destruction by means of lies. In both of these texts a pronounced contrast is drawn between the worldlings, who are deceived and will perish, and the faithful, who will be saved by reason of their fidelity to Jesus.

Revelation 13.11–18

Now we come to the beast arising out of the earth, a parody of Christ in the sense that he faintly resembles a lamb (verse 11). Performing great signs and bringing fire down from heaven (verse 13), he is also a parody of the two witnesses in Chapter 11; in this respect he resembles the magicians of Egypt. The Gospels, we recall, have several warnings against false christs and false prophets, who will work wonders.

Furthermore, in a parody of the sign of the living God in Chapter 7, he has his own version of the seal (verse 16). Those without the mark of the beast must suffer economic sanctions (verse 17). Political idolatry, in other words, has an important mercantile dimension, to which the Book of Revelation will return in later chapters. The adoration of the statue (verse 15), of course, is reminiscent of the fiery furnace story in Daniel.

Perhaps the easiest part of this text to discern is the meaning of the number of the beast. Indeed, John tells us that anyone with intelligence can do it (verse 18). For all that, the symbolism of the number is complex. A first mistake in attempting to read this number is that of imagining it as written out in Arabic numerals. This procedure should be dismissed immediately, because our modern numeral system, derived from the Arabs, was unknown to the writers of the Bible.

In contrast, the numeral systems employed in the Bible are based entirely on the alphabet, whether Hebrew or Greek. Because of this, numbers could also stand for words, and a number of codes became possible. One of these, known as gematria, consisted in taking the prescribed numerical value of the various letters (*aleph* meaning one, *beth* meaning two, and so forth) in a name and then working little puzzles with them. There are several examples of this in Jewish works, such as the Talmud, and in early Christian writings, such as *The Letter of Pseudo-Barnabas*. There are also two examples of it in the Sibylline Oracles and two more in the *graffiti* in the excavations of Pompey.

In John's case, his puzzle runs backwards. He gives us a number and expects us to figure out what word or name the number stands for. Obviously there are many possible combinations of letters that will add up to the value of six hundred and sixty-six. Interpreters of the sacred text, however, have been most partial to the Hebrew form of the name, "Nero Caesar," which does, in fact, add up to exactly the number six hundred and sixty-six. There are other possibilities, but this explanation seems the most compelling. The number was thus a reference to Nero, the first Roman emperor who ever undertook the persecution of the Christian Church.

Chapter 14

Revelation 14.1–13

Now we come again to the sealing of the followers of Christ, first spoken of in Chapter 7. With respect to the "following" of the Lamb (verse 4), of course, the image is found also in the Gospels. When Jesus calls on his disciples to "follow" him, the context is the cross. The Lamb to be followed is the Lamb of sacrifice (Mk 8.34–38; Jn 21.18–19).

There are three angels in this text, representing three dimensions of the final age, the proclamation of the Gospel, the judgment of God on the city of man, and the eternal, wrathful exclusion of idolatry. First, the angel of the everlasting Gospel (verse 6), whose mandate, like the mandate at the end of Matthew, is directed to all nations. These are all called to repentance and conversion to the true God (verse 7; cf. Acts 14.15). Remember that in John's view, the judgment of God is *now*. The judgment of God takes place in the very proclamation of the Good News (cf. Jn 3.19; 18.37). The Gospel here is called eternal; it is the proclamation of the eternal mind of God, his eternal purpose of salvation, the "Mystery" of which the Epistle to the Ephesians speaks.

Second, the angel who proclaims the fall of Babylon (verse 8). This, too, pertains to the Gospel. In biblical thought, the fall of Babylon means that the true Israelites can now go home, because the exile is over. Babylon is whatever enslaves and alienates the people of God. Babylon is the city of false gods, the city that dares to raise up its tower against the face of God; it is the monument to man's achievements without God. Babylon is the city where men do not understand one another, because each man, as it were, speaks his own private meaning. The downfall of this city certainly is Good News, which is the meaning of the word Gospel. Christians are called to *leave* Babylon (18.4).

Third, the angel who proclaims the eschatological outpouring of God's wrath, to the exclusion of all idolatry (verses 9–11). This text is important because, like certain sayings of our Lord in the Gospels, it insists on the eternity of damnation. Unlike many modern men, the Bible believes that the definitive choice of evil lasts forever.

Revelation 14.14–20

On the image of harvest as judgment, see Joel 4.13–14 (3.9–14). The Son of Man on the cloud is, of course, from the Book of Daniel, an image that Jesus interprets as himself in each of the Synoptic Gospels.

Unlike ourselves, men in antiquity actually experienced harvesting with a sickle and treading grapes in a vat, both actions characterized by a distinct measure of violence. Even these relatively benign images of harvest season, therefore, strongly suggest that the "end of time" will be more than slightly daunting. It should not surprise us that the harvesting with a sickle and the trampling of a wine vat are associated with the feeling of God's definitive wrath.

The association of anger with the treading of the grapes was hardly new (cf. Is 63.1–6), and it will appear again (Rev 19.13–15). The grape harvest arrives in September, as the seasonal period of growth comes to an end. It is natural to think of death at this time of the year.

The amount of blood in this text (verse 20) is rather dramatic. The Greek στάδιον being six hundred and seven feet, sixteen στάδια is about two miles. A horse's bridle is about five feet off the ground. Thus we are dealing with a great deal of blood. This must be one of the most unpleasant passages in the New Testament.

The rising pool of blood becomes a kind of Red Sea. Indeed, the following chapter will be full of imagery from the Book of Exodus: plagues, the cloud of the divine presence, the tent of testimony,

Moses, the crossing of the Red Sea, and the destruction of the pursuers.

Chapter 15

Revelation 15.1–8

This shortest chapter in the Book of Revelation introduces the imagery of the seven bowls of plagues, which will be poured out in the next chapter.

The ocean of blood, with which the previous chapter ended, has now become a kind of Red Sea (verses 1–3), which also inserts the theme of the Exodus. This theme itself is appropriate to the outpouring of the plagues. Other components of the Exodus theme likewise appear in this chapter: the Song of Moses, the cloud of the divine presence, the tent of testimony, and so forth.

The "sea of glass" (verse 2) we have already considered in Chapter 4. Beside this sea stand God's people who have passed over it in the definitive Exodus. They are musicians—harpists to be exact—identical with the one hundred and forty-four thousand whom we saw with the Lamb in the previous chapter; there was harp music in that scene too. These elect have "overcome," the very thing to which John had called the seven churches in Chapters 2–3. They are now beyond the power of the beast to harm them.

John sees in heaven the tabernacle of testimony from the Book of Exodus, the traveling tent of the divine presence that Moses and the Israelites carried through the desert. This tent, however, is "heavenly," which means that it is the original model, the very pattern that Moses copied (Ex 25.9, 40; Acts 7.44; Heb 8.5).

Since the tent is a place of worship, we are not surprised that John sees seven angels coming out of it, clothed in priestly vestments (verse 6; cf. Ex 28.4; 39.29), very much as Jesus was clothed in the inaugural vision (Rev 1.12–13).

The tent itself is full of the cloud of the divine presence, the very cloud that led the Israelites through the desert of old. When that tent was dedicated in the desert, the divine cloud took up residence within it (Ex 40.34–38). That cloud later took residence in Solomon's temple (I Kgs 8.1–12), where Isaiah beheld it (6.1–4). In prophetic vision Ezekiel saw that cloud return to the second temple built in 520–16 (Ez 44.4).

The hymn in verses 3–4 should be compared with Solomon's prayer at the dedication of the temple, as recorded in 2 Chronicles 6.14–42. Both prayers, to begin with, are offered "at the sea" (verse 2; 2 Chron 6.12–13). Both prayers thank God for his mighty works, invoke his righteous judgments, and request the conversion of all the nations. Finally, in response to each prayer, fire comes down from heaven (verses 5–8; 2 Chron 7.1–2).

Chapter 16

Revelation 16.1–9

Three of these four plagues are right out of the arsenal of Moses. Sores on the flesh of the bad guys (verse 2) were his sixth plague. As in the account in Exodus, the intent of this plague is that the idolaters should repent, but in neither case does it happen. The second and third plagues here (verses 3–4)—the changing of water into blood, are identical to Moses' first plague—which was regarded, we recall, as a rather *easy* plague, in the sense that even Pharaoh's magicians could do it (Ex 7.22).

Here in Revelation, these two plagues are related to the great bloodshed of persecution caused by the enemies of God's people (verse 6; 16.5–7). This crying out of the altar puts one in mind of the earlier scene where the souls (that is, the blood) of the martyrs cried from the altar (6.9–10). In that earlier scene the saints prayed for justice to be done on earth, for the righteousness of God to be vindicated in history. Now, in the present instance, the voice from the altar praises God that such justice has been done, that God's fidelity has been made manifest.

The fourth plague does not appear in Exodus at all; Moses had been able to blot out the sunlight, but not even he was able to make the sun hotter. Even this plague, nonetheless, does not bring the idolaters to repentance (verse 9).

Revelation 16.10–21

The final three bowls of plagues stand parallel to two other biblical texts: the plagues of Egypt in the Book of Exodus and the trumpets from earlier in the Book of Revelation.

The darkness of the fifth bowl (verse 10) corresponds to the ninth plague in the book of Exodus (10.21–29). The sixth bowl, the drying up of the Euphrates, includes the proliferation of frogs, which corresponds to Moses' second plague against Pharaoh (Ex 8.2–6). The hailstones that accompany the seventh bowl (verse 21) are parallel to Moses' seventh plague against Egypt (Ex 9.13–26).

There are also parallels between these three bowls of plagues and the three final trumpets that appeared earlier in Revelation. Thus, the fifth bowl (verse 10), like the fifth trumpet (9.1–2) causes darkness over the whole earth. The sixth bowl (verse 12), like the sixth trumpet, brings forth an invading army from east of the Euphrates (9.12–19). Finally, at both the seventh bowl and the seventh trumpet there are bolts of lightning, peals of thunder, and an earthquake (verse 18; 11.19).

The sixth bowl of plagues here is a composite. There is, first of all, a drying up of the Euphrates, so that the Parthian armies can march westward. This puts one in mind of the "drying up" of the Jordan, so that the Israelites could move west against the Canaanites. Because of the great difference between the two instances, however, this symbolism should be read as an example of theological "inversion" (in the sense used by John Steinbeck, who often employs biblical symbols in this way), so that the identical image is used for both good and bad meanings. With respect to the drying up of the Euphrates, John knew a precedent in Jeremiah (50.38), who spoke of the drying up of the waters of Babylon, to facilitate its capture by the Persians. Indeed, John will have a great deal to say about the fall of Babylon.

Verse 15 contains a well-known saying of Jesus, in which he compares his final return to the coming of a thief in the dead of night. This dominical saying is preserved in the Gospels of Matthew (24.43) and Luke (12.39).

The final battle takes place at Armageddon (verse 16), which literally is "hill of Megiddo." Megiddo sits on the edge of the Plain of Esdralon and was in antiquity the site of two famous battles, in each of which a king was killed. In Judges 5 the Canaanite king Sisera was slain there, and 2 Kings 23 describes the death of Josiah there in 609. In John's mind, Armageddon symbolizes disaster, catastrophe, and violence.

Chapter 17

Revelation 17.1–6

John's vision of the woman on the scarlet beast is better understood if one bears in mind certain features of his cultural and religious memory.

First, Israel's prophetic tradition had fought against ritual prostitution, one of the standard religious practices of Canaanite religion, which Israel's prophets for centuries struggled to replace. This tradition frequently spoke of idolatry under the metaphor of fornication, a metaphor further suggested by the prophetic perception of Israel as bound to God by a spiritual marriage. This perception is well documented in two prophets of the eighth century, Hosea and Isaiah.

Second, a century earlier Elijah had opposed the immoral cult of Baal, which was sponsored by the Phoenician princess Jezebel, the wife of King Ahab. For this reason, Jezebel came to personify, in Israel's memory, the witch, the wicked woman of loose morals. As in the instance of Naboth's vineyard, as well as the death of many prophets, she was also remembered as a woman responsible for the shedding of innocent blood; Elijah complained that she had put a price on his own head. All of this has been on John's mind; he has already described a certain woman at Thyatira as a Jezebel (2.20–23). The memory of Jezebel is certainly part of the picture of John's image of the woman on the scarlet beast.

Third, Israel's wisdom tradition, especially as found in the Book of Proverbs, spoke of Wisdom as a man's true bride, with whom he was to spend his whole life in intimacy. Opposed to this bridal wisdom was the "loose woman," Dame Folly, personified in the prostitute. This opposition undoubtedly arose from the simple observation that a good marriage to the right woman teaches a man, if he is teachable, how to conduct his life well and wisely, whereas that same man is brought to ruin if he consorts with a meretricious woman. The whore, then, was as bad a figure in Israel's wisdom literature as she is in the prophetic literature.

Fourth, John also seems influenced by certain infamous and profligate women in the more recent history with which he was familiar. In the previous century, for example, there had been the famous *femme fatale*, Cleopatra, while in his own lifetime John knew of Herodias, whose success in murdering John the Baptist surpassed even Jezebel's efforts against Elijah.

Even more recent to John's time there was Berenice, the daughter born to Herod the Great in AD 28. If any woman of John's era could be seen as a whore of international fame, it was Berenice, whose activities we know chiefly from the historian Josephus. By the year 48 she had been widowed twice, once from her own brother, to whom she bore two children. For several years she lived in incest with another brother, Agrippa II, in whose company we find her at the trial of St Paul in Acts 25.13, 22–23; 26.30.

Shortly after this, Berenice was married to King Polemo of Cilicia, but she did not stay long with him. During this period of her life she was mocked by the poet Juvenal.[11] Later on, according to Tacitus and Suetonius,[12] she was the mistress of Titus, who was obliged to abandon her in order to become emperor, Dio Cassius tells us.[13] When John described a "loose woman," in short, none of his readers were at a loss to know what sort of woman he had in mind.

Fifth, the woman in this vision is certainly the personification of the city of Rome, sitting on her seven hills. John did not have to personify Rome; it was already done by Rome's political endorsement of the goddess "Roma," in whose honor John knew of temples

---

[11]Juvenal, *Satires* 6.
[12]Tacitus, *Histories* 2.2; Suetonius, *Lives of the Caesars*, "Titus" 7.
[13]Dio Cassius, *Roman History* 66.15.

at Ephesus, Smyrna, and Pergamum. In the east, Roma had also been assimilated with certain local and traditional fertility goddesses.

The woman here is not only a whore; she is also a drinker of innocent blood, in the tradition of Jezebel and Herodias, the latter remembered especially in the Asian churches as the one responsible for the death of their beloved John the Baptist. Clothed in scarlet and adorned with gold, she appears as a sort of queen, whom John calls Babylon, much in the style of Jeremiah 51.12–17, a text that must be read in connection with John's vision.

Revelation 17.7–18

We have already seen why the number seven is the symbol of perfection. Now, in the assertion that the seven heads of the beast are "seven hills" (verse 9), the seven is inverted to serve as a parody of perfection and completion; that is, perfect and complete evil. The seven hills are, of course, the seven hills on which the city of Rome sits, the *urbs septicollis*, as Suetonius called it.[14] Classical literature is full of references to this topographical feature of the city.[15] In short, "the woman you saw is that great city" (verse 18). The seven heads also put one in mind, of course, of the mythological seven headed Hydra of many ancient sources, from early Canaanite myths to *The Labors of Hercules*.

When the angel goes on to identify the heads with seven kings (verse 10), the identification is less clear. Various speculations are possible in this respect. For instance, if we count Julius Caesar as the first emperor instead of Augustus, then the sixth "head" in verse 10 would be Nero, whom we know to have been a persecutor of the Christian Church. It is not necessary to be quite so literal, however; it may be the case the seven here is to be taken as a symbol for the whole, much as the seven churches of Asia are symbolic of the whole Church. (After all, there were certainly more than seven Christian

---

[14]Suetonius, *The Lives of the Caesars* "Domitian" 5.

[15]Vergil, *Aeneid* 6.783; *Georgics* 2.535; Horace, *Odes* 7; Ovid, *Tristia* 1.5.69; Martial, *Spectacles* 4.64; Cicero, *Letters to Atticus* 6.5.

churches in Asia at the time. There was the church at Colossae, for instance, to which St Paul wrote an epistle.)

Likewise, it is not necessary to be too specific about the ten horns that represent ten kings in verse 12; it is possible that the image serves no purpose except to remind us of the ten kings in the Book of Daniel, an image we examined earlier. The important thing to remember is that these coming ten kings will finally destroy Babylon/Rome itself (verse 16). That is to say, the demons ultimately destroy those who work for them.

Verse 14 speaks of the war between the beast and the Lamb. Lambs generally do rather badly in combat with beasts, causing us to recall that Jesus conquered evil by being defeated by it. All Christian victory involves the cross.

Chapter 18

Revelation 18.1–8

This chapter deals with the city of sin, Babylon. It is not a prophecy of the downfall of Rome, such as that of AD 410 for instance, but an affirmation of hope for the downfall of what the pagan Roman Empire stood for.

In this vision a bright angel is seen; the very earth is illumined by his brightness. He appears with a message of concern for everyone who suffers oppression. His message (verse 2) is a direct quotation from Isaiah 21.9, and the imagery reminds us of the overthrow of Sodom and Gomorrah. The overthrow of this city is related to its place in the world of economics and commerce (verse 3), which John sees to be idolatrous (cf. Col 3.5).

John's complaint against the economic and commercial idolatry of his time should be regarded against the background of the Bible's prophetic literature, especially the prophecies of Amos and Isaiah, who spoke out frequently against the unjust practices of the business world that they knew: price fixing, monopoly, widespread unemployment, and so forth. Actually, such considerations are among the most common in the Bible.

John exhorts believers to get out of Babylon (verse 4), with a direct quotation from Jeremiah 51.45. In that latter text the Jews were being exhorted to flee Babylon so as not to share in that ancient city's peril. "Going out of" a place in order not to share its destruction is a theme that appears rather often in Holy Scripture. One thinks of Noah and his sons "getting out" by building the Ark, for instance. Lot and his family are led out of Sodom by the angels, and the Israelites flee Egypt, and so forth. In Chapter 12 the woman in heaven was given two eagle's wings so that she could *flee to the desert*, and in the Gospels Jesus tells his disciples to flee Jerusalem prior to its destruction. The spiritual message in all this is that those who belong to Christ must put some distance between themselves and those elements of existence that are inimical to man (cf. Jn 17.6, 11, 14–16).

Revelation 18.9–24

And why is the fall of Babylon so bad? Because it is bad for business! Babylon's overthrow means very low profits on the stock market. Verses 12–13 list various products that won't sell any more. The "futures" in frankincense and chariots are down by sixteen points, and the shekel is in free fall!

Everyone calls it a "crisis," and they are right. In fact, John uses the Greek word κρίσις ("judgment") to describe it (verse 10). The crash, when it comes, comes quickly, in a single hour (verses 10, 17, 19). John says that those who weep over Babylon do so from a distance (verse 10). That is, Babylon has mourners, but no helpers. At this final hour of her career, no one will stand with her. No one wants to be associated with her. She was part of an order in which true friendship had no place. It was an order founded on shared interests and profits, not on love. Babylon is bewailed, not for herself, but for her lost investments. In short, the fall of Babylon is bad for business, and John borrows heavily from Isaiah 23 and Ezekiel 27 in order to describe her plight.

We observe that John does not see Babylon fall. An angel tells him that it has already happened. John, that is to say, has no violent vision. There is no projection, here, of a vindictive spirit; it is, rather, the divine resolution of a cosmic problem. The fall of Babylon is not seen; it is revealed to John in a vision of light. John is not interested in revenge but in justice, in the setting right of the world order, and the right order of the world requires the overthrow of Babylon and idolatry, and materialism, and the hedonism for which Babylon stands as a symbol. Her fall is particularly related to her shedding of blood (verse 24). Babylon is thrown into the sea like a stone (verse 21). She is swallowed up in her own chaos (cf. Jer 51.60–63; Lk 17.2, 24–30).

John particularly notes the loss of musical instruments and technology, components of human life first devised by the sons of Cain (Gen 4.17–30). Indeed, there has often been something a bit ambiguous about such music, morally considered. When King Nebuchadnezzar employed "the sound of the horn, flute, harp, lyre, and psaltery, in symphony with all kinds of music" (Dan 3.5, 7, 10, 15) for his idolatrous purposes, it was not the last instance when instrumental music served to deflect men from the worship of the true God. In fact, nonetheless, God designated musical instruments as appropriate to his own worship in the tabernacle and the temple. And, once again, in the Bible's final book heaven resonates with the sounds of trumpet and harp, whereas the damned are forever deprived of such music! The sinful descendents of Cain, the very inventors of harp and flute, will never hear them again.

Chapter 19

Revelation 19.1–10

The previous chapter spoke of the destruction of Babylon, pictured as a woman dressed in scarlet. The present chapter speaks of a contrasting woman, dressed in white, who is called the Bride. A wedding is planned. There is no vision of the Bride just yet, however, nor does John specifically identify her. He will see and describe her in Chapter 21.

We begin the chapter with the "Alleluia." Although our own experience may prompt us to associate that fine prayer with the sight and scent of lilies, here in Revelation it resounds against the background of smoke rising from a destroyed city. The worship scene portrayed here is related to victory over the forces of hell. The word "avenge" at the end of verse 2 reminds us there is a principle of vengeance built into the theological structure of history, for the judgments of God are true and righteous. Sodom and Gomorrah come to mind when we read of this smoke ascending for ever and ever. The worship becomes so warm at verse 6 that Handel decided to set it to music.

By portraying the reign of God as a marriage feast, John brings together three themes, all of them familiar to the Christians of his day. First, the kingdom of God as a banquet, such as we find in Isaiah 25.6. Jesus interpreted the banquet, however, as a marriage feast (Lk 14.15–16). John stresses readiness for the feast (verse 7), much as we find in the parable of the ten maidens at the beginning of Matthew 25.

Second, the marriage theme itself, as a symbol of the union of God with man. We find this theme in the prophets (most notably

Hosea, but also Isaiah and Jeremiah) and the New Testament (e.g., Eph 5.32). The Lamb, who is the groom here, has already been identified earlier in Revelation.

Third, the theme of the garments, which now become the clothing required for attendance at the feast. John has appealed to this imagery several times already (3.4; 6.11; 7.14). The identification of the white garments with righteous deeds puts one in mind of the parable in Matthew 22.11–13.

Revelation 19.11–21

The chapter continues on a different theme: warfare (verses 11–21). Jesus, pictured before as the Lamb, is here portrayed as a warrior on a white destrier. The emphasis is on his vindication of justice, the motif with which the chapter began. He is called "faithful and true," adjectives referring to him in 3.14. These adjectives should be considered especially in the context of martyrdom. That is to say, when a person is about to die a terrible death for the name of Jesus, "faithful and true" are the words he needs to know with respect to Jesus. Like the martyrs, Jesus is here clothed in white. His eyes (verse 12) are flames of fire, much as in John's inaugural vision (1.12–16). His garment (verse 13) is spattered with blood, a detail we saw in 14.18–20. The literary inspiration of this portrayal is the canticle in Isaiah 63.1–3.

One of the Christological titles found here is "king of kings and lord of lords," a title going back to the ancient Assyrian emperors, who were kings ruling over other kings. John tells us that this title appears on the thigh of the Rider on the white horse (verse 16). The thigh here is the place of the scabbard, where the sword hangs. It was common in antiquity to speak of the thigh as the place of the sword. With regard to Achilles, for example, Homer wrote. "And anger came on Peleus's son, and within his shaggy breast the heart was divided two ways, pondering whether *to draw from his thigh the sharp sword*, driving away all those who stood between and kill the son of Atreus, or else to check his spleen within and keep down his anger."[16] The same idiom is found in the *Odyssey* 11.231 and the *Aeneid* 10.788.

The exact idiom is likewise biblical; "Gird your sword on your thigh, everyone of you," commanded Moses to the Levites (Ex 32.27). The expression occurs twice in Judges 3 and in Psalms 45.3 (44.3). Finally, in the Song of Solomon there is a description of the sixty valiant men around the king, "each with his sword upon his thigh, against alarms by night" (3.8). The title on the Warrior's thigh, then, is inscribed on his scabbard.

The sword itself, however, is described as coming forth from his mouth, as in John's inaugural vision in the first chapter. This image, of course, identifies the sword with the word, as in Hebrews 4.12 and Ephesians 6.17. The image of God's word as a sword seems to have been very common among the early Christians, so we are not surprised to see it here. The Rider himself is called "the Word of God," in the only instance of this expression with reference to Jesus outside of the beginning of John's Gospel.

The summoning of the scavenger birds in verse 17 is reminiscent of Ezekiel 39, which describes the defeat of the armies of Gog. We will say more about this battle scene in Ezekiel in our discussion of Revelation 20.

[16]Homer, *Iliad* 1.188–192.

Chapter 20

Revelation 20.1–6

The most controversial part of this passage is the "thousand years," to which several references are made. In order to prepare ourselves to understand John here, it may be useful to reflect on the literary image of the thousand years already well known to John. In the Judaism of John's time there was the popular belief that the Messiah would reign on the earth a thousand years (as there was, more recently, in Hitler's fantasy of a "thousand-year Reich"). This popular belief is extant in Jewish literature of the time, such as *The Testament of the Twelve Patriarchs* and some sayings of famous rabbis. We also find a variation on this theme in the Dead Sea scrolls, which speak of the just who live a thousand generations.

John's description of the Messiah reigning with his loyal followers for a thousand years seems in large measure inspired by Daniel 7, in which God is portrayed as a very old man, the "Ancient of Days," who would take the authority from the fourth beast and give it to God's holy ones, those who are suffering persecution for his sake (Dan 7.9–10, 22, 26–27). The early Christians were fond of this passage, because Jesus had identified himself as the Son of Man, who appears in this same scene in Daniel (7.13–14).

We note that Daniel 7 speaks of "thrones" in the plural, which Christians understood to mean that they too would take part in the judgment of the beast. In other words, they too would sit on thrones along with the Messiah (Mt 19.28). (Indeed, St Paul would apply this idea to a practical ethical question that arose in the early Church, in 1 Corinthians 6.1–3). To say that the believers will judge does not mean, of course, that they will judge in the same sense that God does, because only God has access to the depths of the human heart.

Nonetheless, there is a true and genuine sense in which believers stand in judgment with Christ over history. In the Holy Spirit they are given to know which elements of history are good, and which bad; they are given to discern those components of history that are of value in the sight of God, and those that are not. That is to say, the disciples of Christ are forever passing true judgment over history. They are already on their thrones with the Messiah. The final judgment, at history's end, will simply reveal that they were, all along, the authentic judges of history.

This, then, is their thousand years' reign. It is that area of Christian experience in which Christians are already seated in the high places with Christ (cf. Eph 2.6), already on their thrones, already judges of history. They are said to reign because they are not slaves to the beast and its image. Their reign, nonetheless, is not yet complete, because they still have ahead of them the battle with Gog and Magog.

Revelation 20.7–15

Gog was already well known to readers of Ezekiel 38–39, who would scarcely have been surprised to hear of him, for it was the name of a person from the somewhat recent past. The Hebrew name "Gog" (or Gug) corresponds to the Assyrian "Gugu" and the Greek "Gyges." He was a famous seventh century king of Lydia in Asia Minor, who had died in 644. Accounts of the original Gog are found in Assyrian annals and *History* of Herodotus.

The name is not especially important for the identification of the invader; like the other names in these chapters of Ezekiel, it symbolizes evil realities much larger and more menacing than their historical references. Thus understood, Gog and his forces appear here in Revelation 20. "Magog" appears to be an abbreviation of the Hebrew *min-Gog*, "from Gog." Here in Revelation he is a derived ally of Gog, much as, elsewhere in the book, one beast shares his authority with the other beast in 13.4.

In verses 11–15 everything testifies to its own contamination by "fleeing" from the throne of God. In Chapter 4 John had seen that throne as the origin of all things, and now he sees it as the arbiter of history. Everything flees before it. This is the final judgment, and it belongs to God alone. Here we meet once again the image of the "Book of Life" that appeared earlier in 3.5; 13.8; 17.8.

Chapter 21

We now come to the final two chapters of John's book of prophetic visions. Now we see no more battles, no more bloodshed, no more persecution. John sees, rather, the holy city, New Jerusalem, as the ultimate reality that gives meaning to all that preceded it.

In this final vision, which lasts two chapters, John is aware that *seven* things are gone forever: the sea, death, grief, crying, pain, the curse, and the night (21.1, 4; 22.3, 5). Here we are dealing with the definitive abolition of conflict, the end of chaos. The first symbol of this chaos is the sea, which has only such shape as it is given from outside of itself. The sea represents the nothingness out of which God creates all things, conferring meaning upon them. This chaos is both metaphysical and moral. It represents a nothingness replaced by the lake of fire, the second death. The sea is the hiding place of the monster and the setting where the scarlet woman is enthroned. This sea disappears at the coming of the new heaven and the new earth.

If we take the earth to represent man's empirical and categorical experience, and heaven to represent man's experience of transcendence, then the appearance of the new heaven and the new earth means the transformation of all of man's experience. All of it is made new. The grace of God in Christ does not sanctify just a part of man's existence, but his whole being. Man is not a partially redeemed creature. Both his heaven and his earth are made new.

Both heaven and earth are part of God's final gift to man, the New Jerusalem, the "dwelling of God with man." This dwelling, σκηνή in Greek and מִשְׁכָּן (*mishkan*) in Hebrew (both, if one looks closely, having the same three-letter root: *skn*), was originally a tent made of "skins," as the same etymological root is expressed in English. During the desert wandering after the Exodus, this tent of skins was the abode of God's presence with his people. Indeed, sometimes the word was simply the metaphor for the divine presence (verse 3). For instance, in Leviticus 26.11 we read, "I will set my מִשְׁכָּנִי (*mishkani*) among you. . . . I will walk among you and be your God, and you shall be my people."

Revelation 21.14–27

All of history is symbolized in two women, who are two cities. We have already considered the scarlet woman who is Babylon/Rome. The other woman is the Bride, the New Jerusalem, whose proper place is heaven, but who also flees to the desert, where she does battle with Satan (Chapter 12). Now that battle is over, however, and she appears here in her glory. That other city was seated, as we saw, on seven hills, but this New Jerusalem also sits on a very high mountain, which everyone understood to be symbolized in Mount Zion (cf. Ez 40.1–2). John's vision of the gates of the city is reminiscent of Ezekiel 48.

John's vision here, especially verses 19–21, is also related to Ezekiel 28.12–15, where we find joined the themes of the mountain and the precious stones, for this city is also the Garden of Eden, where those stones first grew (cf. Gen 2.10–12).

The symbolic number here is twelve, which we already considered in Chapter 12, where it was the number of the stars around the head of the heavenly woman. The identification of twelve stars with twelve stones is obvious in our own custom of birthstones to represent zodiacal signs. The symbol is not only astrological, however, but also historical, because it is the number of the patriarchs and apostles. Here, in fact, the twelve gates bear the names of the twelve tribes, who are the seed of the twelve patriarchs, while the twelve foundation stones of the city are identified as the twelve apostles.

We recall that one hundred and forty-four thousand—the number of the righteous—partly involves squaring the number twelve. In the present chapter John stresses that the plane geometry of the holy city is square, as in Ezekiel 45 and 48. John goes beyond Ezekiel, however, in viewing the New Jerusalem as a cube, as in the Holy of Holies of Solomon's temple (1 Kgs 6.20).

Chapter 22

Revelation 22.1–11

The biblical story begins and ends in paradise. Thus, in John's vision of the river of paradise we remember the four-branched river of paradise in Genesis 2. Both here and in Ezekiel 47.1–12 there are monthly fruits growing on the banks of the river, twelve in number, obviously. Just as Adam's curse drove the whole human race out of paradise, so the leaves of the paradisiacal tree of life are for the healing of all the nations.

The theme of the living waters is very much central to the Johannine corpus (cf. Jn 4.7–15; 7.38; 19.34; 1 Jn 5.6–8).

Heaven, portrayed here as vision and worship with the angels (verses 8–9), is for all those whose foreheads are sealed with the mark of the living God. This sealing, of course, stands in contrast to the mark of beast. (It is curious to note that, outside of the book of Revelation [7.2–3; 9.3–4; 13.16–18; 14.1.9; 17.5; 20.4], the word "forehead" does not appear in the New Testament.) The literary background of John's sealing is apparently Ezekiel 9.1–4.

The urgency of John's message is indicated by the command that he not seal it up for future generations. The Lord's coming, in fact, will be soon, and it is imperative for John's readers to "get out" the message. John's visions are not sealed, concealed, esoteric codes to be deciphered by future generations. John clearly expects his own contemporaries to understand what he is writing. These things "must shortly take place" (verse 6); it will all happen "soon" (1.1, 3). John is warning his contemporaries that a special moment of judgment and grace is upon them and that they had better prepare themselves for it, because it is later than they think.

Revelation 22.12–21

This final chapter of Revelation resembles the first chapter of the book in several particulars, one of which is that in both places Jesus speaks to John directly. In both chapters he is called the Alpha and the Omega (verse 12; 1.8). As in that first chapter, likewise, the references to Jesus' swift return (verse 7, for instance) do not pertain solely to his coming at the end of time; he is saying, rather, that in the hour of their trial those who belong to Jesus will find that he is there waiting for them. The blessing in verse 7, therefore, resembles the blessing in 1.3.

In this book a great deal has been said about the worship in the heavenly sanctuary. Now we learn that Christians already share in the worship that the angels give to God (verses 8–9).

Verse 11 indicates a definite cut-off point in history, which is the final coming of Christ. Verse 12, which quotes Isaiah 40.10, promises the reward, which is access to the Holy City, eternal beatitude—the fullness of communion with God. In preparation for that reward, verses 14–16 are something of an altar call, an appeal for repentance, based on all that this book has said.

In referring to those "outside" the City, John is relying on an ancient eucharistic discipline of the Church, called "excommunication," which literally excluded the person from receiving holy communion.[17] One of the major problems of the Christian Church, in any age, is that of distinguishing itself from the world, and the Christian Church, like any institution in history, finds its identity threatened if it does not maintain "lines" that separate it from the world. In early Christian literature, beginning with the New Testament, we find the Church insistent on making those lines sharp and clear. This preoccupation is what accounts for the rather pronounced "us and them" mentality that we find in the New Testament. It is an emphasis essential to maintain if the Church is to preserve her own identity down through history.

---

[17]Cf. *Didache* 9.5; Justin Martyr, *First Apology* 66.1.